The Comple
Photobool

CW00376080

The Complete Photobook

Ron Spillman

FOUNTAIN PRESS LIMITED

Fountain Press Ltd.
65 Victoria Street
Windsor
Berkshire SL4 1EH
England

First published 1969
Second Impression 1970
Second Edition 1971
Second Impression 1972
Third Impression 1972
Fourth Impression 1973
Fifth Impression 1974
Third Edition 1983

ISBN 0 86343 010 4 (Cased)
ISBN 0 86343 020 1 (Limp)

Printed and bound in Spain by
Graficromo S.A. Cordoba

Contents

emphasis 173 Other techniques 173 Linear correction 173 Adding a sky 175 Printing through screens 175 Pseudo-solarisation 175 Lith printing 175 Bas-relief prints 176

19 Processing Colour Films   Page 177

Money, time, and effort 177 Colour negatives 177 Chemical kits 177 Step-by-step processing 178 Slide films 179

20 Colour Printing   Page 181

Description of negative and paper emulsions 181 Filtration systems 182 Colour analysis 183 Chemicals and papers 183 Colour processing equipment 184 Maintaining temperature 185 Making a print 187 Setting up a session 189 The test print 190 Corrective filtration 190 Exposure correction 190 The finished print 191 Prints direct from slides 191

21 Projection   Page 193

Projection equipment 193 Semi-automatic projectors 195 Magazines 196 Fully automatic projectors 196 150w or 250w? 197 Lenses for projectors 198 Projector lamps 198 A-V facilities and techniques, equipment for projection screens 199 Presenting a show 200 Harmony 201 The commentary 201

22 Filing   Page 204

A simple filing system 204 Black & white Negatives 204 Colour and black & white prints 204 Retrieval 205 Filing slides 206

A Word In Advance

The Complete Photobook first appeared in 1969. Its last impression, extensively revised, was in 1974. Since that time, photography has made giant strides, and to keep the reader abreast of these the book has been completely re-written.

Our approach to photography has changed, too. Automation of cameras and darkroom equipment has given us confidence. We no longer bite our nails while waiting to see whether our pictures come out; we expect them to, and usually they oblige. Colour printing is now a straightforward process which should intimidate no-one. Even the novice can go blithely forth with his computerised flashgun to produce excellent bounce-flash colour slides. There is no magic—other than the magic of creativity—in producing first-class colour and black & white photographs. It has been my aim to provide a clear and economical guide to the methods and processes of amateur photography.

The amateur is faced with a daunting choice of cameras, equipment, materials and processes, and hopefully these chapters will help him select the most suitable for his purposes. Techniques and processes have been described, and recommendations made. Such things as time/temperature tables for endless lists of films and developers have been omitted. The makers' instructions are usually best, and, in any case, these are constantly changing.

If *The Complete Photobook* helps you towards better picture-making I will be well satisfied—and thank you for joining me in these pages.

Ronald Spillman, A.I.I.P.

1.
How The Camera Works

You can walk into a camera store today and buy a camera for the price of a few hundred cigarettes. You can also put down the equivalent of a deposit on a house. Naturally, there is an enormous difference in sophistication between the simplest and the most advanced instruments, and yet the differences are not as great as might be imagined. Basically, a camera–any camera–consists of a light-tight chamber with the film at one end, the lens at the other, and a means of letting the light in for a specified amount of time. Although the most expensive camera has vastly more facilities than the cheaper one, the requirement is identical.

If you wanted to take only one picture, you wouldn't need a camera at all. You could get by nicely with an old shoe box or even a corn flakes carton. All you would have to do is to put a piece of film in at one end, and use a darning needle to drill a fine hole at the other end. This would have to be done in a dark room. Then, you put a strip of black insulating tape over the pinhole and sally forth to take your picture. The box would have to be rested on a wall or other firm support for the few minutes (or just a second or so with very fast film) while you peeled back the black tape to make the exposure, and replaced it afterwards. That's all. Then you could go back to the darkroom and develop your film.

The kind of box camera we see in old pictures of our grandparents was little more than a pinhole camera. It had a simple glass lens that projected a reasonably sharp image on to the film and, instead of a strip of black tape, a simple spring-loaded blade that flipped across the lens and let the light in for about 1/25sec. At the other end the film was passed between rollers with a winder, and there was a window so that you could count each frame of film as you wound it

on. Because the exposure was faster, the camera could be hand-held.

The descendant of the simple box camera is the 110 camera which, in its simplest form, is similarly equipped, though there are far more advanced types that will take sharper pictures.

All the gadgets you find on today's advanced cameras are developments from that basic requirement. Lenses that pass more light and give much sharper images. A means of focusing the lens accurately. Shutters that cover a variety of speeds, allowing you to photograph fast action as well as more static subjects. Built-in exposure meters that work out the correct amount of exposure and automatically control the size of the lens opening, or the shutter speed, or both. Facility for interchanging lenses, to permit a greater variety of effects than you can get with a single lens.

It will be a good idea to examine these various facilities and controls one at a time, which will help you understand how they work together. Just as important, it will help you understand the true value of the specification used in advertising the various types of camera on the market.

Shutters

There are two kinds of shutter in general use. One is called a front-lens, or compound, shutter, because it is fitted between the various elements of the lens itself. It consists of a series of concentrically-arranged, spring-loaded blades. Such a shutter normally opens from the centre outwards, until the various blades reach the circumference of the lens, then close again. The simplest types give a single speed, nowadays in the region of 1/50sec. The more advanced types are controllable over a range of speeds from about 1sec to 1/500sec.

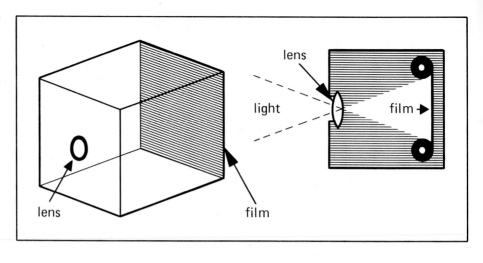

A box camera demonstrates the basic principles: (*1*) a lens projects the image on to the film; (*2*) a shutter controls the duration of exposure. Camera sophistication consists of devices to focus accurately and set the right exposure.

lens

light

lens

film →

lens

film

The complex cross-section of a single-lens reflex, in which the brightness of the image is internally metered. This is called TTL (through-the-lens) metering. The user matches a needle with an index. In more advanced models, shutter speed or aperture, or both, are set automatically.

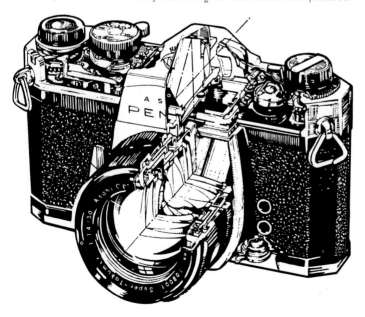

The other type of shutter, fitted to the majority of advanced cameras, is of the focal plane type. Essentially, it is a pair of blinds or blades situated immediately in front of the film, i.e., almost in the focal plane, hence the name. When such a shutter is released, the first blind or blade traverses the film frame, followed automatically by the second. This causes a slot to pass across the film, exposing each part of the film identically. Duration of the exposure is controlled by the speed of traverse coupled with the width of the slot. Naturally, the more tension applied to the shutter springs, and the narrower the slot, the faster the exposure.

The standard focal plane shutter can give speeds of 1sec to 1/1000sec, though a few more modestly-priced cameras may start at $\frac{1}{2}$sec and finish at 1/500sec.

More advanced focal plane shutters have speeds up to 1/4000sec and will expose automatically down to 4sec, 8sec, or even more.

In the more advanced forms, both front-lens and focal plane shutters have a 'B' setting, deriving from ancient days when the shutter was operated by a rubber bulb release. This allows you to open and close the shutter for 'short time' exposures. Press the release and the shutter opens, let go and it closes. Most front-lens shutters and a few focal plane shutters still have a 'T' setting (Time). Press and let go, the shutter remains open. Press again, and the shutter closes. This can be useful when working indoors with very slow film calling for long exposures, as you don't have to stand there holding the release while the exposure is taking place.

Both kinds of shutter also have contacts permitting them to be synchronised with either flashbulbs, flashcubes, magicubes or electronic flash. This will be described in Chapter Thirteen.

Aperture, diaphragm, stop

These are three different words meaning almost the same thing. Whatever type of shutter is fitted to the camera, of front-lens or focal plane type, there is a diaphragm incorporated in the lens mount. It consists of a series of curved blades arranged concentrically. When the diaphragm is 'stopped down' by means of an external control ring, a tiny hole is left at the centre of the lens. When the diaphragm is 'opened up' the blades move outwards until the opening is the full size of the lens. By varying the aperture, we control the brightness of the

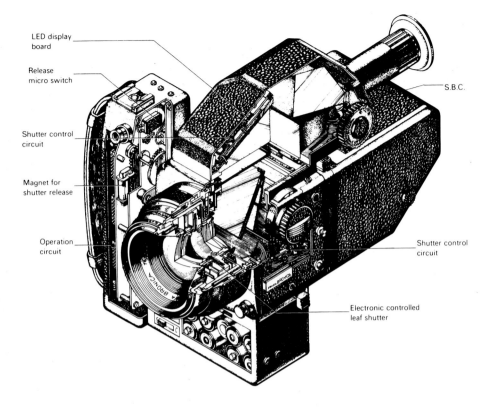

Cross-section of the Zenza Bronica ETR, which has 6x4.5cm format. The camera has auto metering with an electronically-controlled leaf shutter.

LED display board

Release micro switch

Shutter control circuit

Magnet for shutter release

Operation circuit

S.B.C.

Shutter control circuit

Electronic controlled leaf shutter

image reaching the film. These apertures are marked in f/ numbers on the external control ring. The larger the aperture, the smaller the f/ number, which can be a bit confusing for the beginner. Most modern cameras have lenses with a maximum aperture of f/1.4 or f/1.8, though even faster lenses are available, and stop down to a minimum aperture of about f/16, though some telephoto lenses stop down further than this. Here is the typical progression, with each value admitting half, or twice, the amount of light of the previous one. Remember, f/1.4 is largest and brightest, f/16 smallest and dimmest:

f/1.4 f/1.8 f/2.8 f/4 f/5.6 f/8 f/11 f/16

Although the speed of exposures is set by the shutter, people speak of lenses with a maximum aperture of f/1.4 or f/1.8 as being 'fast'. Even though a great many amateur photographers buy cameras fitted with such fast lenses, they seldom use the maximum aperture. A press photographer may occasionally use an aperture of f/1.4 outdoors, to photograph a moving subject in very dull light. The large aperture would allow him to use a fast enough shutter speed to arrest the action. However, such exposures are not noted for good quality

results, and in such conditions he would probably be using flash.

Very large apertures are more useful indoors, especially at night with tungsten lighting. Then we can use a fast enough shutter speed to arrest moderate action and preserve natural atmosphere. Even so, many photographers will prefer to use bounce-flash (q.v. Chapter 13), which also provides a natural-looking effect. Of course, large apertures are essential when photographing a subject such as cabaret, if the effect of the stage lighting is to be preserved.

Lens apertures and shutter speeds work together in an arithmetical progression. For example, 1/60sec at f/11 provides exactly the same exposure to the film as 1/30sec at f/16, or 1/125sec at f/8, and it is the correct choice of any combination that often puzzles the novice but he should not let this worry him. The choice becomes easy if we base it on the subject requirement, giving preference to the faster shutter speeds for action subjects, and preference to the smaller f/ stops if we want our subject to be sharp from close to the camera right back to the far distance. This latter requirement is known as depth of field, and will be dealt with next. Here is a progression of shutter speed/aperture com-

subject. Incidentally, the f/ number for the maximum aperture of a given lens is arrived at by dividing the focal length of the lens by the diameter. The focal length is the distance between the nodal point of the lens (somewhere between the various elements) and the film, with the lens focused at its Infinity setting, divided by the diameter. Thus, a 50mm lens with a diameter of 27.7mm has an effective maximum aperture of f/1.8, while an f/1.4 lens of the same focal length would have a diameter of 35.7mm. Knowing this probably won't help you take better pictures, but I include the information for those who are technically-minded.

Depth of field

Depth of field refers to the zone of sharp focus in a picture on either side of the subject you have focused on. That is, towards the camera, and beyond the subject. The smaller the aperture used, the greater the depth of field. The larger the aperture, the shorter the depth of field. Depth of field is also controlled by the distance of the subject focused on. The farther away the subject, the greater the depth of field for any given aperture. The closer the subject, the smaller the depth of field for the same aperture. This can be seen on pages 14–15 where zone focusing is also demonstrated. Zone focusing is a useful idea that helps you take pictures quickly without the necessity for re-focusing the lens for every single picture. Choice of a given aperture and distance setting means that everything within a given range will be satisfactorily sharp. Zone focusing is useful only with the standard lens on your camera or with wideangle lenses. This is because, for any given aperture, depth of field decreases the greater the focal length of the lens. For example, if you use a 35mm camera with a standard lens of 50mm, focus on a subject at 5m, with an aperture of f/8, depth of field will extend from 3.37m to 9.77m. Using the same aperture of f/8 with a telephoto lens of 105mm and focused on the same distance of 5m, depth of field would extend from only 4.47m to 5.67m. This isn't always a disadvantage, as we shall see in the section on Interchangeable Lenses, in Chapter Two.

To sum up:
1. The greater the aperture, the shorter the depth of field for a given distance.

In the classic twin-lens camera, two lenses of identical focal length are used. The viewing lens projects an image on to the focusing screen by way of an inclined mirror. Below this, the film receives an almost identical image from the taking lens.

binations all of which would provide the same amount of exposure:

aperture:	f/1.4	f/1.8	f/2.8	f/4
	at	at	at	at
shutter:	1000	500	250	125
aperture:	f/5.6	f/8	f/11	f/16
	at	at	at	at
shutter:	60	30	15	8

The shutter speeds, of course, are expressed as fractions of a second. When you have read the following section on depth of field you will know how to choose the right combination for a given

2. The greater the distance focused on, the greater the depth of field for a given aperture.
3. The longer the focal length of the lens, the shorter the depth of field for a given aperture and distance.

Most camera and lens manuals give depth of field tables, listing the depth of field at all apertures and at distances up to the Infinity setting, beyond which everything is sharp. Such tables are of technical value, particularly when photographing extremely close subjects, but need not be referred to in your general out-and-about photography. If you have a single-lens reflex, where you can actually observe the depth of field effect in the viewfinder screen, the tables are not necessary. If you have a fixed-lens camera (one which can be focused, but which will not take interchangeable lenses) the focal length will be somewhere between 35mm and 50mm, and this will give good depth of field at moderate apertures and distances beyond two or three metres. Again, the tables are not necessary, and after you've seen the results of your first one or two films you'll have a working idea of depth of field.

Hyperfocal distance

This is a term you may come across, which refers to a method of pre-setting the focus on a lens so that everything beyond a given point will be sharp. It is the basis on which zone focusing has been devised. The hyperfocal distance for a given lens, and aperture, is based on the focal length of the lens and the degree of sharpness we are prepared to accept as satisfactory. It should be remembered that there can be only one point of true focus in any photograph, and only at this point will the lens be projecting the sharpest image of which it is capable. The depth of field on either side of this point is merely a zone of *acceptable* sharpness, that is, satisfactory to the eye.

To make use of hyperfocal distance, you need to refer to the depth of field table supplied with your camera or lens, or to the depth of field scale engraved round the lens mount itself. Take, by way of example, a 50mm lens which we intend to use for well-lit outdoor subjects, and we choose a moderate aperture of f/8. Reference to the depth of field table or scale shows that if you set the lens at Infinity, everything from about 10m will be sharp. 10m is the hyperfocal distance. If we now focus, not on Infinity, but on this hyperfocal distance, everything from half this distance to Infinity will be sharp. In this case, it means everything beyond 5m from the camera. This can be very useful when photographing scenery which includes subject matter a few metres from the camera, simply because

There is a reciprocal relationship between shutter speeds and lens apertures. Each larger aperture passes twice as much light, while each faster shutter speed reduces the exposure by half. Thus, 1/125sec at f/8 gives the same overall exposure as 1/250sec at f/5.6, or 1/500sec at f/4. The aperture is reduced by a bladed diaphragm.

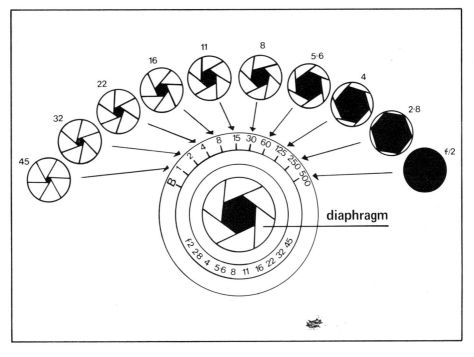

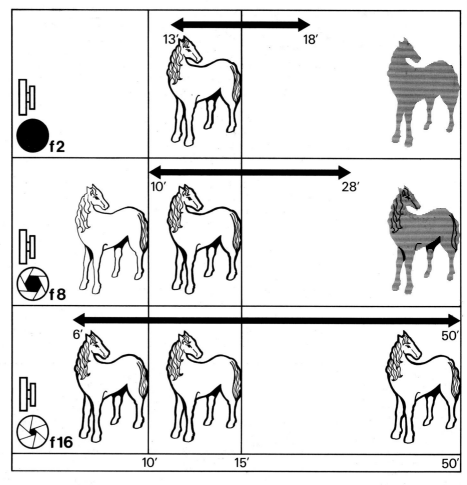

the camera can be raised to the eye without the necessity of re-focusing.

The lens

Too many beginners confuse 'faster' with 'better' when it comes to selecting a lens. The speed of a lens is only part of the story, and it is a fact that a great many photographers have never used their lens at its maximum aperture. All the same, advertisers often infer that faster is better – it is certainly more expensive – whereas the sharpness, or definition, of the lens is probably of more importance.

Naturally, lens quality varies from maker to maker. There are high quality lenses from the top makers and a host of lenses of lesser quality made for the less discerning end of the market. One cannot make hard and fast rules about lens quality, but in general it can be stated that an f/1.8 lens from a top manufacturer will give a slightly better performance *at any aperture* than an f/1.4 lens from the same stable. However, nowadays the differ-

ences tend to be marginal, and the overall performance of lenses of extremely large aperture is excellent. Only with a moderately priced range of lenses might one expect a markedly better performance from an f/1.8 lens than from an f/1.4 lens.

The same was not always the case, and because many older cameras can still be bought second-hand, it is worth noting the difference. For example, forty and fifty year old lenses made for early Leicas and Contaxes usually had a maximum aperture of f/2, which is virtually the same as the f/1.8 lens today. These lenses were considered very fast, as indeed they are. Both makers also supplied an f/1.5 'speed' lens, neither of which was as sharp, or had as much contrast, as the f/2. Consequently, the faster lenses were only chosen for subjects such as theatre and cabaret, or outdoor photography at night. The Leica also had an f/3.5 lens, and the Contax an f/2.8 lens, both of which had better definition and contrast than the f/2 or

14

f/1.5 versions. In fact, in those far off days f/3.5 was considered quite fast enough— and even with our much faster lenses today, most of our pictures are taken at even smaller apertures. Such lenses, attached to beautifully made cameras dating from a time when there was no built-in obsolescence, still perform as well as modestly-priced lenses today.

One area in which the modern lens scores is in the introduction of lens coating. A microscopically thin film of a substance such as magnesium fluoride is vacuum-coated on the air/glass surfaces of the lens, and this has the effect of reducing reflection as the image-forming light-rays pass through. In the latest forms of coating, as many as seven or more coatings may be applied at each surface, the effect being to give a brighter image with better contrast, less chance of flare, and richer colour saturation when using colour film.

The glass from which lenses are made is quite soft. Thus, your lens should be dusted only occasionally, by means of a soft brush. If a few specks of dust refuse to shift, use special lens cleaning tissues which are available at every camera store, stroking the glass only lightly with a circular motion. Tissues should also be used if the lens is accidentally smeared with grease or a finger print. Finger prints are acid and if left too long will actually etch the delicate glass. They will certainly destroy some of the coating.

There are two kinds of lens cleaning fluid available. One is intended only for viewfinders, slides, plastic and so on. The other kind is for optical lenses. But, never use the former on a coated lens— which nowadays means all lenses—as it will cause smears. If you have inadvertently applied this fluid to your coated lens, get it off with a lens tissue moistened with water.

Interchangeable lenses

The beginner in single-lens reflex photography has an enormous range of wide-angle, telephoto and zoom lenses to

Zone focusing helps you get into action fast. Using a standard lens, (a) focus set to about 7ft will give an area of sharpness from approximately 6 to 9ft; (b) focus set to 12ft will cover about 9 to 16ft; (c) provided a small aperture is used for distant and middle-distance views, the camera may be set at infinity. With an autofocus camera, manual focusing is not necessary.

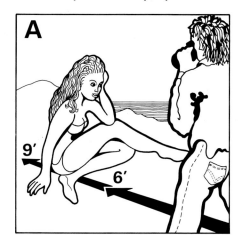

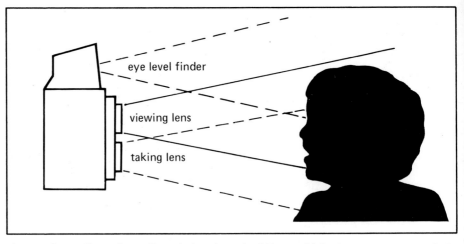

eye level finder

viewing lens

taking lens

choose from. Sometimes the choice is solved for him, as he buys a 'special offer' outfit consisting of the camera with standard lens, plus one wideangle and one telephoto. Usually the wideangle is 28mm focal length, and the telephoto 135mm. This, in fact, is quite a good choice. However, many ranges of lenses include focal lengths of 8mm, 15mm, 16mm, 18mm, 21mm, 24mm, 28mm, 35mm, 50mm (standard), 85mm, 105mm, 135mm, 200mm, 300mm, 400mm, 500mm, 1000mm, and a number of intermediate, as well as even longer, focal lengths. How to make a sensible choice?

First of all, any given focal length might be ideal for a particular job, but that does not mean that we need a large number of lenses. Just one wideangle and one telephoto are sufficient for the beginner, and indeed, many skilled photographers possess no more than that. In practice, the more lenses you own, the less pictures you take, simply because so much time and effort is consumed in

deciding which lens to use, and in changing to it.

At one time, 35mm was considered quite wideangle, but this focal length has been replaced in popularity by the 28mm. You certainly do not need both. The more extreme wideangles, of 24mm and even wider, are great for impact, but are less often useful than the 28mm. At the other end of the scale, both 85mm and 105mm are considered ideal for a head-and-shoulder portrait, but again you don't need both. The 135mm has long been considered the ideal compromise, giving good magnification for distant views, while at the same time providing a full-face portrait without too much flattening of perspective effect. The beginner whose main interest is portraiture, should choose the 85mm or 105mm, which is also a good landscape lens, while the 135mm should be chosen if the main interest is in landscape. The longer focal lengths are much more difficult to hand-hold, and should be bought only for such subjects as sport, and then only after the 135mm has been mastered.

Zooms

A zoom lens can be adjusted over a range of focal lengths, and therefore replaces a number of prime lenses. Popular zooms are 35–105mm, 70-150mm, 80–210mm, though there are many others. Because of modern computer technology, zoom lenses now approach the optical quality of prime lenses. A camera outfit consisting of a 28mm, 50mm standard, and zoom 80–210mm, is all that most photographers would ever require.

Used at its maximum focal length, a zoom handles almost as well as a prime lens of similar focal length. At its shortest

Different apertures are suitable for different subjects. When fast shutter speeds are needed in dim light, a wide aperture is called for. With static subjects in bright light, a smaller aperture is sufficient and gives more depth of field.

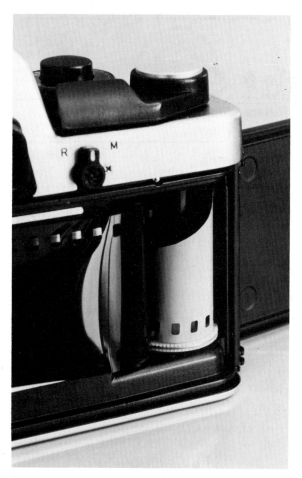 

focal length, however, it is far bulkier, and more difficult to hold still, than a prime lens. Also, the maximum aperture of a zoom lens is usually smaller than that of a prime lens. This places some restriction on photography in dim light, and the image is more difficult to focus.

On the credit side, the zoom lens is a wonderful teacher. With a prime lens, you normally stand at a convenient distance from the subject, focus and expose, with ot without having altered the distance from the subject in the interest of composition. Wherever you stand with a zoom, you are more likely to try the zoom effect. You soon learn an important lesson—that impact often increases as the subject proper becomes larger in the frame, and extraneous background detail is eliminated.

A diagram showing the angles of various focal lengths is on page 34.

18

2.
The Right Camera

Choosing your first camera, or moving up from your first simple camera to a more advanced type, can be an expensive business, especially if you choose wrongly, or are given the wrong advice. This chapter has been written to help you make the right choice, and spend only as much as is necessary for your requirements. If the advertisements are to be believed, you have to buy the 'best', which usually means the most expensive, in order to produce high quality pictures, and that just isn't so. Often, the difference between cameras costing £150 and £450, is simply that the latter are designed for the kind of rugged use, day in, day out, that only a professional news or sports photographer would ever submit his equipment to.

Choosing correctly is more a matter of deciding on the right type of camera than the right model. There are any number of medium-priced single-lens reflex cameras on the market, all capable of producing results as good as can be obtained with the most costly Nikon or Leica. What really matters, is whether a single-lens reflex, or some other type of camera, is better for your kind of photography. To take an extreme example, why pay hundreds of pounds for a single-lens reflex if a £50 pocket camera will serve you better? Let's go through the various types of camera, and discuss the suitability of each for the various kinds of photography.

The 110 and disc

These formats started with the Kodak Pocket Instamatic, which has been copied by a great many manufacturers. They are small, slip easily into the pocket, and produce a tiny negative or slide, a few mm long. If you have no pretensions to exhibition or competition work, the little 110 or disc may be the camera for you.

Most people expose colour negative film in such cameras. Negative films with the suffix 'II', such as Kodacolor II, Fujicolor II and so on, have very thin emulsions and give a sharp image, and these should always be chosen. Provided the tiny camera has a good lens, is properly focused and exposed, and held quite still while the shutter release is being pressed, these tiny negatives will produce excellent colour enprints, about

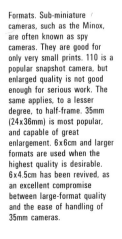

Formats. Sub-miniature cameras, such as the Minox, are often known as spy cameras. They are good for only very small prints. 110 is a popular snapshot camera, but enlarged quality is not good enough for serious work. The same applies, to a lesser degree, to half-frame. 35mm (24x36mm) is most popular, and capable of great enlargement. 6x6cm and larger formats are used when the highest quality is desirable. 6x4.5cm has been revived, as an excellent compromise between large-format quality and the ease of handling of 35mm cameras.

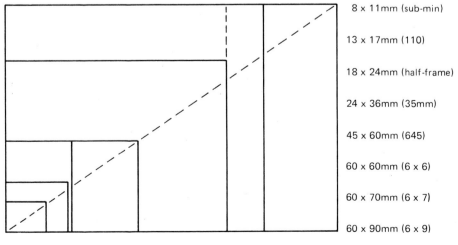

8 x 11mm (sub-min)

13 x 17mm (110)

18 x 24mm (half-frame)

24 x 36mm (35mm)

45 x 60mm (645)

60 x 60mm (6 x 6)

60 x 70mm (6 x 7)

60 x 90mm (6 x 9)

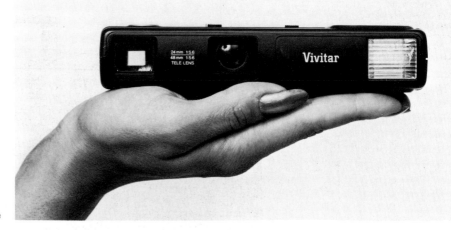

A modern 110 camera, pocket sized, with built-in electronic flash.

The latest disc cameras automatically switch on the flash when needed. The film is advanced automatically, and the lithium battery lasts about 5 years.

4 × 5in. These are ideal for carrying about in wallet or purse, to show to family and friends. There are special projectors for 110 slides, although ordinary 35mm slide projectors can be used. However, don't expect to get a good screen image greater than about 2 × 1½ft. This, of course, limits the audience for a slide show to just a few people.

There are special fast colour negative films now available, with a speed rating of 400 ASA (Chapter Three). These enable pictures to be taken in dull light or indoors, even where there is a certain amount of action going on, but some older types of 110 camera will not accept 400 ASA cartridges. Before buying these faster films, make sure that your 110 is compatible with them.

The simplest 110 has a lens with a small maximum aperture, a single shutter

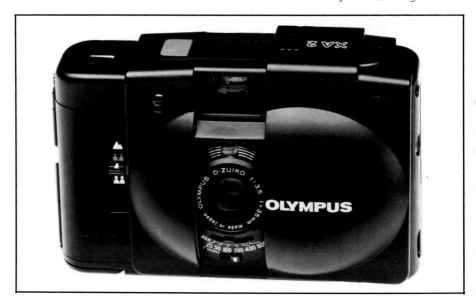

A fully automatic 35mm compact, in which shutter and aperture are interlinked. Fastest in use, but with no manual override.

The first totally decision-free 35mm camera with total electronic control. The flash operates for fill-in or full illumination, focus is infra-red auto, and there is full LED readout in the viewfinder.

speed of about 1/60sec, and a lens which cannot be focused. Because of the extreme depth of field of 110 lenses, usually about 25mm, the subject matter will be *sharp enough* from about 6ft to the far distance, or Infinity.

As you go up the price scale, there are many extra refinements. These include automatic metering, wide-aperture lenses that can be focused by scale or rangefinder, built-in electronic flash, and even zoom lenses, for wideangle or telephoto effects. At least two major manu-

facturers have produced a 110 which is a scaled-down version of the full-size 35mm single-lens reflex, complete with interchangeable lenses and motor wind.

In general, it should be remembered that however expensive a 110 or disc may be, it is not the instrument for serious work. This is partly because the tiny negatives or slides cannot stand a great amount of enlargement. It is also partly because of the optical limitations. Subjects close to the camera may look fairly sharp in a big enlargement (big means about 5×7in in the case of 110), while objects in the middle distance will be less sharp, and really distant objects will have no detail at all. This is due to the inability of lens and film to resolve fine detail at a distance.

The Compact

Compact is the name given to a pocketable camera taking 35mm film and producing negatives or slides 1 × 1½in (24 × 36mm). The compact does not have the interchangeable lens facility of the single-lens reflex, and is thus more limited in its scope. However, a great many photographers today find that a compact camera does everything they want it to. With the majority of compacts, it is true to say that within their limitations results equal those which can be obtained with an SLR.

Because the compact does not have the complex design of the SLR, it is altogether simpler to produce, and the

Many SLR cameras now have an auto-winder that locks on to the baseplate and automatically winds on the film after each exposure. The usual rate of operation is about 2 frames per second.

An auto-winder permits a rapid sequence of pictures. This little girl running was captured in about 5 sec, using an auto-wider on an SLR.

benefits are twofold. First, the price of a good compact is far lower than that of most SLRs, and second, the compact does not go wrong so often. Repair costs are high, so this is a factor well worth considering. The SLR is a complicated instrument. The fault rate is far higher than most manufacturers would like to admit, and if you are unlucky enough to have the camera go wrong after the usual one year guarantee period has run out, well, the repair estimate may make your teeth chatter.

Spillman's First Law: cameras become fault-prone the day after the guarantee period expires.

Compacts can be divided into three

basic types: manual, automatic, and automatic with manual override. The average manual compact has a lens which can be focused by scale, or distance symbols, from about 3ft to Infinity beyond 30ft. The most modestly priced has a built-in exposure meter, but the lens aperture and shutter speed must be set by the user, according to the meter's indication.

The fully automatic compact has the meter interlinked with a combined aperture/shutter mechanism. When aimed at the subject and the shutter release

Many photographers are now using a short zoom instead of the standard lens. This is the popular Nikon FE, fitted with a 35-70mm f/3.5 Zoom-Nikkor.

A stereoscopic attachment and viewer for a 35mm camera.

Used by top professionals because of its ruggedness and high quality, a Nikon F3 with motor drive.

The waterproof 35mm Nikonos III, which can be used under water without a special housing.

receding from close to the camera into the far distance, a small aperture can be combined with a slow shutter speed. Conversely, for a fast-moving subject a fast shutter speed can be combined with a larger lens aperture.

Compact cameras have moderately wideangle lenses, of 35–45mm focal length, compared to the 50mm standard lens of the SLR. With a wideangle lens, depth-of-field is greater, and this often covers up inaccurate focusing. For this reason, and also because of economy in a competitive market, makers of cheaper compacts are often content to incorporate just a distance scale, or symbols such as a head-andshoulders, a half-length couple, a group of two people full-length, and a mountain peak (silhouettes). This system works quite well for middle distance subjects on a bright day, even though the user may have a 50 per cent focusing error. In the case of a dull day and a portrait close to the camera (a situation calling for a wide lens aperture) focusing is far more critical, and an auto-focus model is much to be preferred.

Truly accurate focusing calls for the inclusion of a rangefinder. As you look through the viewfinder and focus the lens, a pair of images come together in a central spot or rectangle. When they coincide, the subject is accurately focused. Rangefinders are incorporated in many compacts, not only the most expensive, and some serious photographers prefer them to autofocus models.

As the compact camera takes standard cassettes of 35mm film, a very wide range of emulsions is available for it, ranging from the slowest black & white film to the fastest colour. In this respect, the compact user is at no disadvantage *vis à vis* the single-lens reflex user. The main drawbacks of the compact are (a) at the closest focusing distance of 3ft a portrait tends to have exaggerated modelling, so it is best to try for nothing closer than a half-length, and (b) like the 110 or disc it is not suitable for extreme close-up work, for which the SLR is ideal.

Some compacts now have built-in flash units and even automatic focusing devices. The former is quite useful, though size limitation means less power (and less covering distance) than when a larger and more powerful flash unit is chosen. The latter has a certain appeal to the casual snapshotter with a love of automation, but is not as critically accurate as a rangefinder–which, after all, takes only a few moments to operate.

depressed, the camera will deliver the correct exposure over a range which is usually from 1/650sec at f/16 down to 1/30sec at f/2.8. Different combinations of aperture and shutter speed cannot be selected. This type of compact is ideal for candids or 'grab shots', especially if autofocus is incorporated.

The automatic compact with manual override is a little more complicated, but gives more scope to the serious photographer, as it will work in either the automatic or manual mode. It is normally used at the automatic setting, and will cope with most subjects. If a certain subject calls for extreme depth-of-field, for example, in the case of a row of trees

The Mamiya C220F twin-lens reflex for 6x6cm negatives on 120 roll film. The front lens panel is interchangeable, complete with its viewing and taking lenses.

Held upside down above the head, the twin-lens camera can be used to compose a picture over the heads of a crowd.

Single-lens Reflex

No one camera is ideal for every job, but the single-lens reflex, known universally as the SLR, is probably the best compromise. Basically, the image formed by the lens is reflected upwards through a pentaprism and is seen by the eye right-way round and rightside up. When the shutter release is depressed, the mirror flies up, the lens stops down automatically to the predetermined aperture, the shutter operates, the mirror drops and the lens opens again to full aperture. The viewfinder image is blotted out for a mere 1/30sec or so. Most important, the image seen by the eye is precisely the same as that which will fall on the film, without parallax error.

Parallax? In most non-SLR cameras there is an optical viewfinder, separated by about an inch from the lens. Lens and viewfinder are on different axes. With distant subjects this does not matter, but in close-up photography, the different viewpoints may cause the photographer to slice off the top of a head. To compensate for this, such viewfinders usually have a pair of parallax marks, guiding the photographer to raise the camera the correct amount at distances of about 3–4ft.

Just as important, the SLR permits the photographer to study the effect of using different apertures, stopping down to increase depth-of-field, or opening up to limit sharp focus to just the subject itself. This is known as differential focusing, especially effective with telephoto lenses.

The main value of the SLR is that interchangeable wideangle and telephoto lenses may be used, to produce a variety of perspective effects. Thus, if you do not feel the need for extra lenses, there is little point in buying a costly SLR. The exception is the photographer who does a great deal of close-up work (insects, flowers, stamps), for which the accurate framing and easy focusing of the SLR is ideal.

Nearly all modern SLRs have through-the-lens metering. The brightness of the image is measured by a cell or cells, and the information used to set the correct exposure. The simplest TTL-metering (through-the-lens) SLRs are of the match-needle type. By adjusting the aperture ring, or the shutter speed, a needle or claw visible in the viewfinder is aligned with the floating meter needle. In automatic cameras, the aperture or shutter

The fashion photographer's favourite, the 6x6cm Hasselblad, here seen fitted with a wideangle lens and a motor drive.

The Hasselblad fitted with a Polaroid back

26

The Rolleiflex SLX above, is an electronic marvel in the 6x6cm format. Exposure and film wind are automatic, and the camera can even be set to take 10 exposures on one frame in 1sec, for shots of golf swings. tennis strokes, and the like. (Top right) A roll film camera with interchangeable lenses that takes negatives 6 x 7cm.

speed is set automatically. There are two basic types, aperture-priority and shutter priority. In the former the user sets the aperture and the camera automatically adjusts the shutter speed. In the latter, the user sets the shutter speed and the camera automatically adjusts the aperture.

Which is better, aperture or shutter priority? This is really a matter of taste. As there are 11 values between 1sec and 1/1000sec, but only 7 values between f/16 and f/1.8, it has been argued that the aperture-priority camera has a big advantage. This is likely to be of value to the novice. After a little practice, any photographer will learn to choose either an aperture or a shutter speed with which the automatic camera can cope. In any case, the exposure readout is visible in the viewfinder of most SLRs, and errors can be instantly corrected with a twist of the aperture ring or shutter speed dial.

Most SLRs work on the open-aperture metering principle. Whether you pre-select an aperture or leave it to the camera, the lens remains at full aperture until the moment of exposure. The advantage is that the bright screen image permits critical viewing and focusing to the last moment. Older SLRs work in the stop-down mode, i.e., the image dims as the lens is stopped down. The only

advantage is that the extent of the depth-of-field can be seen. However, the majority of open-aperture metering SLRs also have a depth-of-field preview button or can be switched to the stop-down metering mode.

In some TTL-metering cameras the image brightness is measured equally across the whole frame (averaging type), in others preference is given to the centre half of the frame (centre-weighted type), while a very few models have an additional switch permitting the reading to be confined to a very small central area (spot type). Any of these types are capable of providing accurate exposure, and it should not be presumed that the spot type is more accurate. It is, in fact, often more difficult to use, and more prone to error, unless handled by an expert. Full details of how to obtain correct exposure are given in Ch. five.

Most SLR viewfinder screens have one or more aids to easy viewing and focusing. First, a fresnel lens is cemented under the groundglass screen itself. This has the effect of spreading the illumination evenly to the edges and corners of the frame. At the centre of the screen there is a circle of microprisms, or a split-image rangefinder, or both. The former is a pattern of tiny prisms which break up the image when not in

The Polaroid Land SX-70 instant camera delivers a dry print in 1½ seconds and the colour develops fully in less than one minute with Supercolor film.

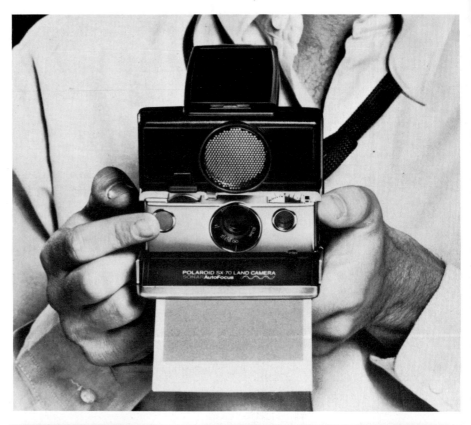

The latest Polaroid cameras have automatic sonar focusing. This is the advanced Model 5000.

focus, but snap into focus when the lens is properly adjusted. The latter is a pair of opposed wedges which divide the out-of-focus image, the two halves coinciding when the focus is corrected.

Both focusing methods work best with lenses of about 28mm to 135mm focal length. With focal lengths shorter or longer than this they do not work well. With the wideangles there is less of a problem, because the extreme depth-of-field of such lenses covers all but the wildest focusing errors. Many photographers simply use the focusing scale.

A firm tripod is a necessity for many serious jobs. About 5 lb is the minimum weight for a rigid tripod.

With extreme telephoto lenses, focusing is best achieved at full aperture, either by using the plain groundglass circle surrounding the microprisms (where this exists), or by using the surrounding fresnel area.

A great many modern SLRs, and compacts for that matter, now have a series of illuminated LEDs (light-emitting diodes) visible in the viewfinder to indicate the shutter speed in use. Previously, and with less expensive models today, the readout depends on illumination received through a tiny window, and this, of course, depends on the brightness of the ambient light. LEDs, on the other hand, can equally well be seen in the dimmest conditions.

The latest SLRs operate not only in manual and automatic modes, but in the programmed (P) mode as well. The camera chooses a suitable combination of aperture and shutter speed.

35mm Rangefinder

The only remaining 35mm non-SLR cameras with interchangeable lens facility are the Leica M4-2, the Minolta CL, the Russian Fed 4L and Kiev models. The Leica is in a class of its own, made to the very highest engineering standards and, naturally, costing a great deal. The 35mm rangefinder couples automatically to lenses of 35–135mm focal length. Shorter focal lengths may be used with a clip-on viewfinder. On the Leica, a Visoflex housing adapts the camera to SLR form, so that extreme telephoto lenses may be used.

In general photography, the rangefinder is more positive than the SLR screen, especially in dim light. For this reason it is preferred by some press photographers, and by many photographers whose vision is weak.

The disadvantage of the 35mm rangefinder camera is that depth-of-field cannot be previewed (exception: Leica/Visoflex with telephoto lenses), though parallax is automatically compensated for, but not corrected, in the Leica viewfinder. Lack of these facilities is not considered a disadvantage by the camera's advocates who point out (a) that with a little practice the effect is easily estimated with standard to medium telephoto lenses, (b) that differential focusing is hardly possible, and seldom required, with wideangle lenses, and (c) both differential focusing and precise framing are possible with the Visoflex.

A great advantage of the 35mm rangefinder camera, Leica and Minolta CL, is the extreme quietness in operation, a mere whisper compared to the relative clank of the SLR.

Larger cameras

It remains true that, other things being equal, better technical quality can be obtained with a larger format than with a smaller one, mainly because of the lesser degree of enlargement required. Popular formats are 4.5×6cm, 6×6cm, and 6×7cm. Two manufacturers, Mamiya and Bronica, have introduced scaled-up SLRs which take 15 frames 4.5×6cm on 120 rollfilm. Classic 6×6cm rollfilm single-lens reflexes are the Hasselblad and that fully-automatic marvel the Rolleiflex SLX. The latter does everything electronically. It winds on the film, makes the exposures, and can even take 10 exposures on one frame in 1sec—ideal for tennis strokes, golf swings, and so on, which formerly required special stroboscopic flash equipment.

There are several 6×7cm single lens reflexes and rangefinder cameras available, which are often preferred by professionals, on account of the large high-quality colour transparency that can be produced for commercial purposes.

There are also a number of 6×6cm twin-lens reflex cameras, in which the upper lens reflects the image upwards via an inclined mirror to a hooded viewing screen, while the lower lens projects a similar image onto the film. The obsolete classic is the German-made Rolleiflex 2.8F with Zeiss Planar f/2.8 taking lens. A rather more modestly-priced copy is the Yashica Mat 124G. However, the 'Rollei' still holds its place as one of the easiest cameras to use, and has been referred to as a complete outfit on a single strap.

The Mamiya twin-lens is heavier and more cumbersome in use although it has the advantage of taking interchangeable pairs of wideangle and telephoto lenses.

Even bigger technical cameras are available for specialist work, in formats from 6×9cm right up to 10×8in and larger, but these do not come within the scope of this book.

3.
The Right Film

Colour prints? Colour slides? Black & white prints? Which do you like best? Some photographers like to try different types of film, while others are content to stick with just one. In this chapter we are going to discuss the various types of film, but let us start with the subject of suitability. A recent survey on the amateur sales of film, which includes film from all makers, was as follows:

black & white	8%
colour negative (for prints)	73%
colour slide	19%

Here's what those figures probably mean. First, the majority of camera owners, most of whom would not call themselves 'serious' photographers, prefer to buy colour negative films, from which colour prints are made. Small en-prints, about 4×5in, are easy to carry around in wallet or purse, for showing to friends and family. The occasional enlargement can also be made. Colour negative films are also bought by serious photographers. Club photographers use them to make exhibition prints, and commercial photographers use them (in 6×6cm or 6×7cm format) for weddings and display work.

As it is quite easy to have a colour slide made from a colour negative, why do we need slide film? First of all, a slide made from a negative is never quite as good as an original slide exposed in the camera. For best quality in projection, and for reproduction in magazines, we just have to use slide film. Only occasionally will an editor be willing to reproduce from a print, and then it has to be a really superior, colourful print on glossy paper. On the other hand, by using reversal colour paper, a print made from a slide can be just as good, but more expensive, than a print made from a negative.

Those survey figures might suggest that black & white is on the way out. Far from it. Black & white film is used by press and other professional photographers, and by many advanced amateurs.

When colour? When black & white?

This is a problem faced by many amateur photographers. The fact is, colour isn't always better. For the majority of snap-shotters, who get great pleasure from recording their holidays and outings, friends, family, and anything that takes their fancy, artistic considerations do not exist. Colour adds a dimension of reality, and their choice is simply between colour negative and colour slide.

When we come to the photographer with artistic aspirations, things are different. Basically, if the kind of pictures you are interested in depend for their effect on the interplay, and fine nuances of, colours, then obviously your choice must be colour film. Make a study of the pictures you see in good magazines, and you will see other pictures which depend for their effect on strength of line, and the juxtaposition of bold masses. Such pictures are often best rendered in black & white, and the introduction of colour would simply detract from the strength. It should also be remembered that black & white reproduction is not so costly, and usually faster, than colour. This is why newspapers are printed in black & white. There is little point in submitting a colour shot, however good, to a magazine or newspaper that cannot use it.

If you intend to work professionally, or at least make some money from your hobby, you will have to suit the film to the job. Examples would be slides for submission to colour magazines and competitions, colour prints for portraits undertaken for payment, and black & white for magazines and competitions that do not want colour.

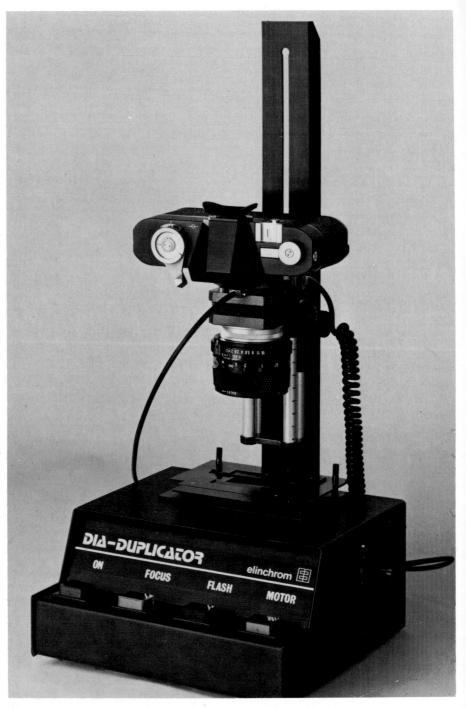

This Elinchrom Dia-Duplicator is used for duplicating slides and negatives in formats from 35mm to 6x7cm. It has a fibre optic control for contrast.

Colour negative

There was a time when an enlargement made from a 35mm colour negative was significantly inferior to one made from a 6×6cm or larger negative. Now we have much improved 35mm colour negative films. These are thinner than previously, giving sharper enlargements.

They are of finer grain, which gives smoother gradation. The colour is better saturated (richer), so greater degrees of enlargement are possible without the colours becoming wishy-washy. Fujicolor HR and Kodacolor VR would have seemed impossible a few years ago.

The best of these have a speed of 100ASA, and are very sharp, with quite

fine grain. There are 400ASA versions, grainier but ideal for dim light outdoors. Kodacolor 1000 is ultra fast, but the grain no coarser than that of older 400ASA emulsions. The difference in granularity is seldom obtrusive on colour prints up to 8 × 10in.

Colour slide

Depending on the laboratory you send your films to, a colour negative may or may not be printed on colour paper made by the same manufacturer. Kodak negatives may be printed on Fuji or Sakura paper, and so on. It is also true that all modern films, from whatever maker, have now achieved very high standards. Add these two facts together, and you will see that there is no great advantage in choosing any particular make of film.

Provided you send your work to a good printer, the results should be satisfactory. You may have to try two or three processing houses before you find one that consistently sends back satisfactory prints, but when you find one stick to it.

With colour slide film matters are different. Slide films from different makers tend to have different characteristics, and there are many 'favourite' slide films. One advanced worker will prefer the beautiful blues and greens of Agfa CT18 or Agfachrome S (the latter is the professional version, but obtainable by amateurs), while another will prefer the ability of Kodachrome 25 to render the finest detail. Professionals who need their films processed quickly may choose one of the Kodak Ektachrome films, especially Ektachrome 200 or 400 for available light work outdoors, or 3M's 640T for indoor work without flash.

The 'standard' speed for slide films is 50-100ASA, which is fast enough for most outdoor work, or for use indoors

33

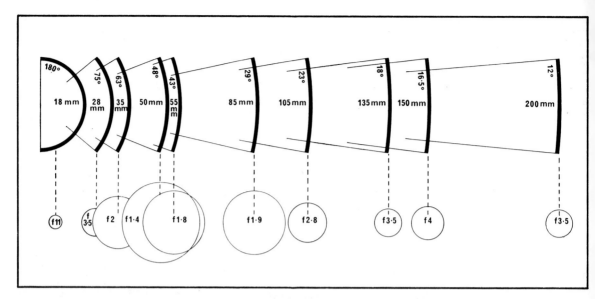

Lenses for 35mm cameras range from fish-eye to extreme telephoto. This chart shows the angles and apertures from one maker's range, though even shorter and longer focal lengths are obtainable.

Tamron lenses have adapters for almost every make of SLR. This range includes wideangles, telephotos, close-focusing zooms, and (in front) a 500mm f/8 catadioptric 'mirror' lens.

The Tamron SP 90mm f/2.5 Tele Macro lens may be used as an ordinary medium telephoto, but will focus right down to 15,4in for 1:2 magnification.

This 2X tele-converter is inserted between the camera and lens, doubling the focal length but reducing the light transmission by the equivalent of two stops. Other converters give up to 3X the focal length, but with three stops light loss. This one is from the Tamron SP range.

Because of its short length, a catadioptric, or mirror, lens, shown top right, is easier to hand-hold than a conventional lens of the same focal length. This is an 800mm f/11 Vivitar Solid Catadioptric telephoto.

This Novoflex follow-focus unit has a spring-loaded trigger, enabling a moving object to be kept in focus. It is shown fitted with a 400m Noflexar lens and shoulder stock.

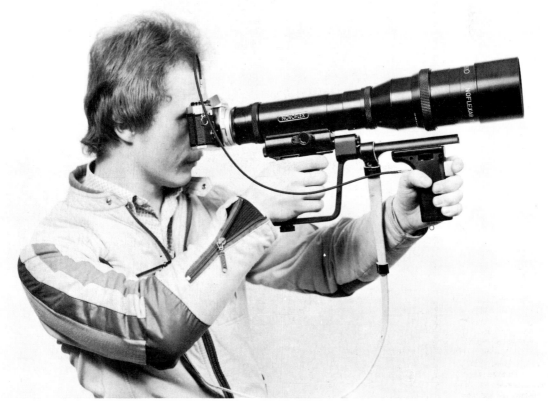

In the picture on the left, the sun shining through the old lamp standard has caused flare in a conventionally coated lens. In the picture on the right, a multi-coated lens has been used.

with flash. Kodachrome 64 is universally popular, but Kodachrome 25, although slower, is recognised as the sharpest, finest-grained of them all. For really detailed work intended for reproduction, it can outperform any of the 120-size slide films.

With slide films of 200–640 ASA available, the amateur can be excused for thinking that the faster the film, the better. This is far from being the case. The general rule should be, choose a film that is fast enough for the purpose, but no faster. Reserve the superspeed emulsions for dim light, fast action, or special effects.

Although the differences between slide films are far less than they used to be, there are certainly characteristic differences, so taste will always play a part. Some textbooks purposely refrain from expressing preferences, but I believe I would be failing in my duty towards the reader if I did not give some practical advice on choice. If you are starting out, it is suggested that you use Kodachrome 64 or Agfa CT18. Having tried one, try the other, and compare the results. You may want to look no further. If you do decide to try other makes, you will be able to compare them with what are undoubtedly two of the popular slide films. Then you can make your final choice.

The characteristic granularity of a film depends on its inherent fineness and distribution of silver halide grains, and to some extent on the type of developer used. Left to right are greatly enlarged sections of the developed image of very slow, slow, medium-speed, and fast films.

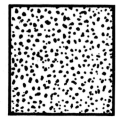 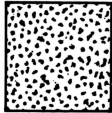  

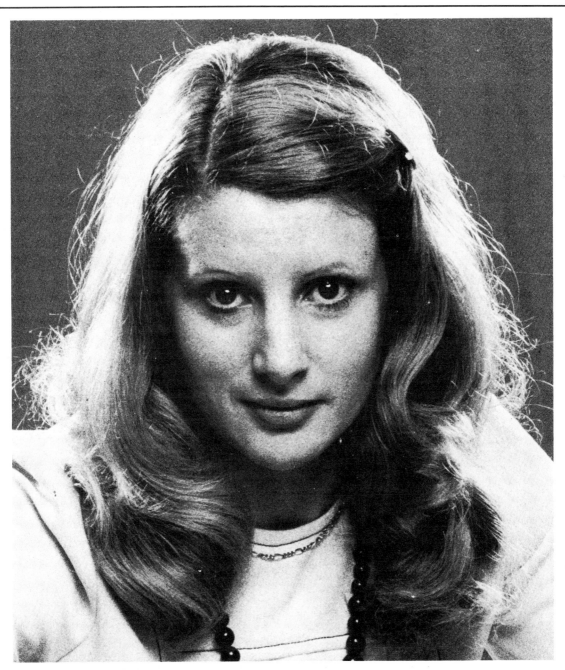

The emulsion of a developed film contains thousands of tiny clusters of metallic silver. The appearance of granularity is most evident when fast films and ordinary developers are used. However, modern fast films have remarkably fine grain, as can be seen in this 15X linear enlargement. Ilford HP5 developed in ID.11.

Pathways to colour

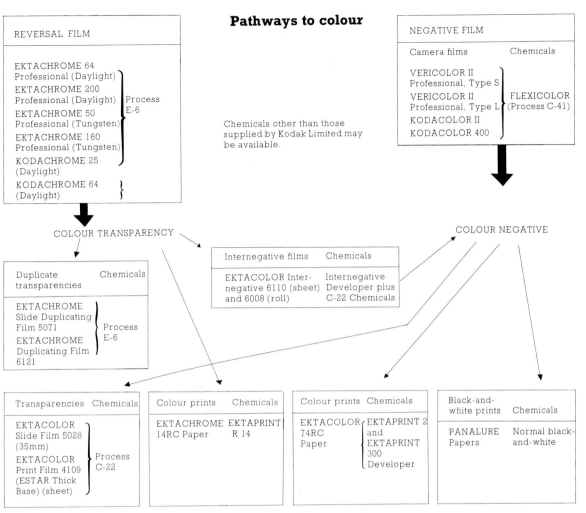

REVERSAL FILM

EKTACHROME 64
Professional (Daylight)
EKTACHROME 200
Professional (Daylight)
EKTACHROME 50
Professional (Tungsten) } Process
EKTACHROME 160   E-6
Professional (Tungsten)
KODACHROME 25
(Daylight)
KODACHROME 64
(Daylight) }

Chemicals other than those
supplied by Kodak Limited may
be available.

NEGATIVE FILM

Camera films	Chemicals
VERICOLOR II Professional, Type S	
VERICOLOR II Professional, Type L	FLEXICOLOR (Process C-41)
KODACOLOR II	
KODACOLOR 400	

COLOUR TRANSPARENCY

COLOUR NEGATIVE

Duplicate transparencies	Chemicals
EKTACHROME Slide Duplicating Film 5071	Process E-6
EKTACHROME Duplicating Film 6121	

Internegative films	Chemicals
EKTACOLOR Internegative 6110 (sheet) and 6008 (roll)	Internegative Developer plus C-22 Chemicals

Transparencies	Chemicals
EKTACOLOR Slide Film 5028 (35mm)	Process C-22
EKTACOLOR Print Film 4109 (ESTAR Thick Base) (sheet)	

Colour prints	Chemicals
EKTACHROME 14RC Paper	EKTAPRINT R 14

Colour prints	Chemicals
EKTACOLOR 74RC Paper	EKTAPRINT 2 and EKTAPRINT 300 Developer

Black-and-white prints	Chemicals
PANALURE Papers	Normal black-and-white

This chart shows how colour and black and white prints can be made from colour negatives, slides from colour negatives, and colour prints or negatives made from slides, with Kodak materials.

Kodak Ektachrome 200 or 400 is ideal for sports shots when high speeds are required in dull weather. Here, the film was uprated to twice the speed, and extra development given.

The photograph on the opposite page was taken on fast colour film by yellowish daylight from the window at the right. The monochrome effect helps create a pattern picture.

Kodachrome film requires very complex processing, and thus can be processed only by Kodak. Other films can be processed by independent laboratories, or even at home. Ektachrome and other E6 process compatible films are used by professionals, partly for this reason, and partly because extra film speed can be obtained by increasing the time in the first developer. The method is described in Chapter Nineteen.

Black & white

In general, the slower the film the finer the grain, the greater the ability to resolve fine detail, and the higher the inherent contrast. Slow films are preferred by pictorial photographers who require the utmost in technical quality in big enlargements, that is, in excess of about 15 × 12in and up to about 30 × 20in.

The choice, however, is by no means arbitrary. Although the slow films (25–50 ASA) give the best technical quality, excellent quality can also be obtained from medium speed films (100–125 ASA). The extra speed makes them most useful for shooting under a variety of lighting conditions, especially if you do not want to carry a tripod for the majority of your work. With correct exposure and careful processing, the increase in grain and the loss of fine resolution is little more than marginal. Thus, the 125 ASA black & white film is the most popular choice, and certainly best for the novice.

The 'standard' fast film is 400 ASA, and there is no doubt that the two most popular are Kodak Tri-X and Ilford HP5. There is hardly a pressman in the world who does not prefer one of these two films to any other make. Considering the speed, the grain is remarkably fine and the sharpness excellent. In fact, again with carefully controlled exposure and processing, it is often difficult to detect the difference from one of the medium speed films if enlargement is not beyond about 10 × 8in.

One advantage of working with 35mm film, is that it is available in a far greater variety of emulsions than larger (or smaller) formats. Very slow copying films can be had in 35mm, which are not available in 120 rollfilm. The 120 rollfilm user has a choice of Kodak Royal-X Pan, with a speed of 1250 ASA, and this is sometimes used by pressmen for such subjects as floodlit stadium sports. The 35mm user has Kodak 2475 Recording film, which may be rated at anything from 1000 ASA to 6400 ASA for photographing that traditional black cat in the coal cellar. Special infra-red films are available in 35mm, both black & white and colour. 35mm film can also be bought economically in bulk rolls, and cut and put into cassettes by the user.

To get the best from 35mm black & white film, you have to know how to choose the right developer for a given emulsion, and this is dealt with in Chapter Seventeen.

Chromogenic Films

A recent development has been the introduction of black and white films which are exposed in the normal way but after development the silver is bleached out, leaving a pure dye image. The advantage of this is that the negative is virtually grainless and will stand much more enlargement than normal films. Another advantage is that, although they are rated at 400ASA, they can be exposed at different ASA ratings on the same film, and development does not have to be forced. Negatives exposed at all speeds between 50ASA and 800ASA on the same film will be printable although varying in density. A disadvantage of these films is that, like most colour films, they have to be processed at a high temperature, usually 38°C (100°F) instead of the more usual 20°C (68°F). They also cost a little more. Two of these films are at present available – Ilford XP-1 and Agfa Vario XL.

4.
Choosing Filters

Once upon a time the choice of a filter was a simple matter. Every photographer used black & white film, and the choice was confined to the colours yellow, green, orange and red. Today, when most people use colour film, there is an enormous array of filters and special effects attachments, as well as the usual filters for black & white. What are they all for, are they truly 'creative', as the advertisements insist, and just how many do you need? For the sake of the novice, let us start with filters for use with colour film, and explain what they do.

Filters for colour

There are two types of colour slide film generally available, one for daylight and one for artificial light use. Daylight type is balanced in manufacture to give natural results when exposed to noon sunlight, with a few clouds in the sky acting both as diffusers and reflectors. Technically, this kind of light is said to have a colour temperature of 5600K, or Kelvin. Just a few words of explanation about what Kelvin means.

If you put a black iron poker in a fire, it begins to glow a dark red, then brightens to bright red, then orange, then yellow, then white, and finally blue. The Kelvin colour temperature scale is based on this fact. Here are some examples, most of which are approximate:

light sources	col. temp. (K)
Noon sun, blue sky, no clouds	12000+
Sun, blue sky and clouds	5600
Blue flashbulbs, electronic flash	5500
Photoflood lamp	3400
500w tungsten studio lamp	3200
100w household lamp	2900
60w household lamp	2760

All you need do, is remember that the colder the light the higher the colour temperature, the warmer the light the lower the temperature. As our daylight-type slide film is balanced for 5600K, it gives a natural effect with light of the same temperature. If we take pictures under an open blue skylight, or move out of the sun into the shade, the slides will look cold, or bluish. To correct this, we can put a slightly yellowish filter over the lens, and back comes that natural sunny effect.

The most useful of all filters for this purpose is the Wratten 1A or 1B, universally called the Skylight filter. It is almost colourless to the eye. This is the only filter used by a great many successful colour photographers, and is probably all you need. Professionals, of course, use a great many more filters to balance the light, but the amateur is well advised not to 'go the whole hog' and equip himself with a series of these. Their use can be confusing.

In the early morning or late evening the sun's rays come obliquely through the atmosphere and the light becomes more reddish, i.e., the colour temperature drops, and the slides have a very warm, or reddish look about them. Because of this, some slide film manufacturers suggest the use of a Wratten 82A (very pale blue) filter within two hours of sunrise or sunset. Although the practice is technically correct, it tends to make an early morning or late evening scene look as though it were taken in noon sunlight, and the effect is out of keeping with the long shadows. Many experienced photographers prefer not to use a filter, and retain the yellowish effect, which, after all, is the attraction of such light.

Artificial light

Colour slide film balanced for artificial light is known as Type B, though Agfa-

It doesn't always do to filter out the blue in a colour shot. The Skylight filter was removed for this picture of the Mountains of Mohr, in Ireland, which are typically cloaked in blue shadows.

Gevaert use different letters. Thus, Agfachrome 50L (long exposure) is for artificial light, while 50S (short exposure) is for daylight. These L films give natural colours when used with 500w studio lamps (Argaphoto), and a quite acceptable result by ordinary household lighting, though a bit on the warm side. With the bluer overrun photoflood lamps the effect is slightly cold, or bluish, but this can be corrected by using a Wratten 81A filter, which is slightly yellowish. This filter is a little deeper in hue than the Skylight filter, and serves also to reduce blue when working with daylight type film in excessively blue conditions. Examples would be at sea under open blue skylight, or high in the mountains, where the light has an excess of ultra-violet.

Conversion filters

These filters make it possible to use daylight type film by artificial light, and *vice versa.* If you use daylight film in artificial light without a filter the results will have an overall reddish colour. This is corrected by using a blue 80A filter with studio lamps or household lighting, and the slightly lighter 80B filter with Photofloods. As the latter are bluer than studio lamps, a less deep filter is necessary for correction. Incidentally, the results are passable for ordinary interiors, but some photographers consider that an unpleasant greenish tinge becomes apparent in portraits, which is probably why Kodak suggest that the 80A or 80B filter in conjunction with daylight slide film should be reserved for emergencies only.

For colour slide photography in tungsten light there is nothing to beat Type B (Agfachrome, L) film. Type B used for daylight photography without a filter would give blue slides. It can be corrected by using a Wratten 85B filter, which is strongly orange. Incidentally, with this combination there is almost total reduction of ultra-violet, so, whatever the weather, it is never necessary to add a secondary filter, such as the Skylight or the deeper 81A.

The few filters so far mentioned are all the amateur is ever likely to need. The Wratten designations have been given, as these are the universally accepted norm, but other manufacturers, notably the Japanese, sometimes give them other names, and these are included in the list below. Fluorescent lighting emits an incomplete spectrum, lacking in red, and

This was taken in a Japanese lake, using a 6-point starburst filter on a compact camera. The brilliant reflection has caused the water to darken, showing up the sun's rays. These would have been lost if the exposure had been modified.

it is not possible to correct this fully. Fluorescent tubes are supplied in a whole range of 'colours' from 'warm white' to 'daylight', and if ever you need to take slides of the highest possible quality by their light, Kodak or Agfa-Gevaert will inform you of the best filtration, provided you let them know the designation of the tubes. In practice, you will find that the Japanese FL-D (fluorescent-daylight) filter gives acceptable results when using daylight type film with almost any type of fluorescent tubes.

1A or 1B (Skylight)	For daylight type film. Prevents bluish slides under blue skylight without clouds, or when working in the shade. May be left on the lens even in sun-and-cloud conditions; also acts as a lens protector.
82A	Also called 'Morning & Evening' in Japanese lists. Removes yellowish quality of light within two hours of sunrise and sunset. Can be used to create a 'blue' mood. Least important of this short list of filters.
80A, 80B	Strong blue filters; converts daylight colour film for use in tungsten light.
85B	Strong orange filter; converts Type B (L) colour film for use in daylight.
81A	Also called 'Cloudy' in Japanese lists. Has a stronger UV absorption than the 1A, useful at sea under blue skylight, for open beaches, and in the mountains. Also used with Type B (L) film under Photoflood lighting.
FL-D	Will give a more natural effect when using daylight type film under fluorescent lighting. Subdues the bluish or greenish hue.

Filters for colour negatives

Colour negative film, like daylight type slide film, is balanced for exposure to daylight, blue flashbulbs, and electronic flash. It is not made in artificial light variety, in amateur sizes. Used in daylight, there is no reason why you should not use the same filters that have been suggested for slide film. This makes the job of the printer easier when you send your films away for processing. However, the use of filters is less critical with colour negative, as the printer can adjust the filtration while making your colour prints.

By all means use a Skylight filter under open blue skylight or when working in the shade. In the rush and bustle of mass production the printer may be concerned only to produce prints of acceptable colour, without too much attention to the subtleties of morning or evening light.

The printer also knows which of your negatives were made indoors under artificial lighting, and can apply filtration to correct the orange appearance. His job is made easier if you use the blue 80B conversion filter under such conditions. Incidentally, all the filters mentioned, apart from the Skylight, cut down the amount of light reaching the film, by anything from $\frac{1}{3}$ stop in the case of the 81A and 82A, $\frac{2}{3}$ stop in the case of the 85B, and $1\frac{2}{3}$ stops in the case of the 80B. If your camera has through-the-lens metering, or a meter cell which will be covered by the filter, exposure will automatically be adjusted. If not, or if you work with a separate meter, study the instructions packed with the filter, and don't forget to apply the filter factor.

Filters for black & white

Apart from special films which are not sensitive to red (orthochromatic), those you buy in the shops for general photography are sensitive to all colours (panchromatic). Even panchromatic films do not see colours with exactly the same tonal values as the human eye, however. The biggest difference is that the film is especially sensitive to blue. We see a blue sky, but the black & white print usually depicts it as white, or a very light grey. This means that there is little or no difference between sky and clouds, which can be disappointing.

This state of affairs can be remedied by using a colour filter. The most popular of these is the 2X yellow, so-called because it has an exposure increase factor of 2. The yellow combines with the blue sky to produce green, to which the film is less sensitive. Thus, our blue sky comes out as a mid-grey, and the clouds show up very well.

An orange filter will give an even darker sky, with greater cloud contrast. It also has a definite lightening effect on brickwork, thatching, and any subject of yellow, brown or red colouring. According to the strength of the orange filter, a factor of anything from 3X to 5X will have to be applied.

A red filter gives even more contrast than the orange. It will blacken a sky, and have an even greater lightening effect on warm-coloured subjects. The effect can be quite dramatic, though the exposure increase factor of 5X to 10X means a much longer exposure which may necessitate the use of a tripod if a slow film is being used. When using orange or red filters, ensure that people's faces are not included close to the camera, as there is an unhealthy lightening effect on skin tones, and even sunburnt faces begin to look anaemic. Orange, and especially red, filters, have a very strong absorption of ultra-violet light. Because of this, they can penetrate a great deal of distant haze. This may be desirable on a very misty day, or when taking military reconnaissance photographs, but for landscape work, beware. If the far hills are just as clear as the foreground, the effect of aerial perspective will be lost.

Orange and red filters also have a darkening effect on foliage. This does not matter if a skyline of trees is shown against the white clouds of a powerful sky, but where an unbroken blue sky reaches the horizon, trees and sky may merge into a single dark tone. Be careful. Study the effect through the filter, as the effect on the eye will be similar to that on the film.

The final filter used in general black & white photography is the green, or yellow-green. Statistics show that less green filters are sold than yellow, orange or red. The proportions, as a matter of interest,are as follows:

Yellow	—	100
Orange	—	50
Red	—	50
Green	—	15

This is strange, as the green filter has an important role to play in outdoor photography. It not only has the property of lightening green foliage, but is able to differentiate fine differences in tone between the various greens of which even a single tree is composed. It is thus an excellent choice when photographing a woodland scene composed largely of foliage. At the same time, it will add about the same amount of tone to a blue sky as a yellow filter, and is the only filter that will retain the tones of suntanned skin. Depending on the make, the exposure increase factor for green or yellow-green filters is from 3X to 4X.

Many serious workers in black & white have all four filters. However, a yellow filter alone will suffice for the majority of your work, with possibly a red for strong dramatisation, and the green if you wish to combine summer portraiture with detailed landscapes.

Effect attachments

Some of these are filters, in that they affect the colour or tone of a colour or black & white picture. Others, which usually come under the heading of 'effect filters', have only an optical effect on the picture. Nowadays, a huge number of effect filters and other lens attachments are on the market, and the amateur can easily be misled into thinking that only by possessing a great number of them can he be creative. Advertisers, in fact, perpetuate this myth by calling some of the filters and attachments 'creative'. Only the photographer can create, though judicious use of some attachments may help.

First come the Starburst filters. These are made of flat optical glass etched with criss-cross lines. Where bright point sources of light appear in the picture, such as the sparkle on water, or the sun itself, the filter causes rays of light to radiate from each point. There are four-, six- and eight-point starbursts. A variation is the cross-screen, with double parallel rays. Some of these consist of two glasses, one of which can be rotated to vary the angle of the rays. The starburst effect can usually be obtained without the aid of the filter, simply by stopping the camera lens down to its smallest aperture.

A variation is the rainbow filter, in which the rays appear in prismatic colours. Another type splits up the whole image into uneven patches of overlapping prismatic colours—I call this one the seasickness filter!

Very popular, and quite useful, are the graduated filters, popularised by the French photographer Jean Coquin, sold as Chromofilters originally, and now part of the Cokin and other systems. These consist of a sheet of optical resin, coloured at one end, and shading off to clear resin. They can be had in grey, blue, tabac, emerald, red, yellow, and several other colours. The most obvious use is to add colour to a blank sky without affecting the foreground colour, but they can be used in many situations to add interest to a fairly colourless subject.

The idea is not original, by the way. In the early '30s, Rollei introduced a graduated yellow filter. Because such filters

45

work best when separated a little from the lens, the Rollei filter was held in a sliding holder that fitted the end of the square lenshood of the Rolleiflex. Modern manufacturers have continued this design.

Other effect filters include several plain colours to give an all-over bias to a colour picture, and dimpled glass to give a romantic soft-focus effect to portraits and views.

There are also a number of way-out filters for colour, under such names as Nebula and Andromeda. These produce geometric, usually circular, patterns of colour bars around points of illumination. To my mind, the emphatic pattern is obtrusive, and has the effect of swamping any pictorial interest in the view itself. Similar, but not quite so way-out, are two- and three-colour filters, which divide the picture into halves or thirds of different colours.

Next we come to the purely optical attachments. The multi-facet types produce more than one image of the subject within the frame, in a variety of geometrical patterns. Examples are three- and five-image circular, and three- and five-image parallel. These are undoubt-edly useful for the professional, who often has to make an interesting image from an uninteresting subject, and judicious use by the amateur can add interest to a slide show – if not repeated too often.

More useful are the centre-spot filters. One type leaves the centre of the image clear and blurs the surrounding area, while another type adds colour to the surroundings. Both are useful in moderation. Fog filters do just that, by overlying the image with an appearance of mist or fog. Be careful when using these, as the degree of fog is the same for the foreground as the distance, which is not the case in Nature.

One other useful optical attachment is the near-far. This consists of half a close-up lens in a circular mount. It allows a distant subject to occupy half the frame, with an extremely close-up subject at the other side, with both in much sharper focus than could be obtained merely by stopping the lens down to increase depth-of-field.

Although most special effects filters and attachments are for colour photography, one should remember that some of them are equally useful in black & white work.

5.
Exposure

A camera which doesn't work out the exposure for you is the exception rather than the rule nowadays. This certainly applies to instruments used by most amateurs. Some photographers, even novices, buy a camera and never have a moment's trouble with exposure. Film after film, all their slides and prints are satisfactory. Well, almost, and the satisfaction is so great that they don't worry overmuch about the occasional shot that is badly under- or over-exposed. Serious workers, however, are not content with this. They want *every* shot to come out well. To achieve this happy state of affairs, we have to go a little more deeply into the question of exposure, and then we shall be able to avoid the few, but annoying, failures.

How the meter works

An exposure meter, whether it is built into the camera or not, is simply an instrument for measuring the intensity of the light. When it is calibrated for the speed of the film in use, the meter reading is translated into a shutter speed/lens aperture combination that will give just the right amount of exposure to the film. A meter can measure the range of brightnesses of a subject far better than the human eye, which rapidly accommodates itself to low or high light levels, and is therefore unable to make really accurate comparisons with a norm. On the other hand, we can think, and the meter cannot.

The fact that the meter cannot think does not matter in the majority of cases. All exposure meters built into cameras, whether they work through the lens or not, use the reflected light principle. This means that they measure the light reflected from the subject. Look at an ordinary view, and you will see a few heavy shadows, a few bright highlights, and a great many half-tones in between.

This is what we call an average subject, and ninety-five per cent of the pictures we take fall into this category. The meter scans the subject, and integrates the various tones. That is, it adds up all the various brightnesses, and provides an average reading. This average reading is designed to produce a mid-tone exposure on the film.

Ninety-five per cent accuracy? That means 34.2 successful frames on each 36-exposure film! We might let it go at that, except for the fact that some of the most exciting lighting effects (and therefore our best pictures) are often among that 1.8 per cent of situations where the lighting is not average.

Non-average subjects

Let us suppose we are photographing a girl in a light dress against a large expanse of dark woodland, the girl occupying only about one-quarter of the frame. The meter scans the scene, decides that it is very dark, and indicates a long exposure to compensate for it. The meter, as we have said, has averaged the various brightnesses and is trying to provide an overall mid-tone exposure. The meter just doesn't understand that the exposure should be correct for the face and the dress, and that the dark background doesn't need any extra exposure – we want it to come out dark, anyway. The resultant exposure, if we are working in colour, puts unnecessary detail in the background, and the figure is too light, with thin, washed-out colours. In this case we have to override the meter, and give less than the indication.

There are several ways of doing this. The easiest, and most accurate, is to approach the subject more closely, until the meter's angle of acceptance is confined to the face and perhaps part of the dress. Then, fix this exposure before

returning to the shooting position and taking the picture. This reading may be half or less than the indication when the whole scene was included. Another method is to raise the camera a little to include more of the sky, or turn it towards an area similar in tone to the important part of the subject, then fix the exposure. A more arbitrary method is simply to reduce the exposure by guesswork, probably by half or one stop. A useful procedure is given shortly.

Now let us take the other extreme, where the surroundings are much brighter than the important part of the subject. A classic example would be two or three colourfully dressed skiers crossing an expanse of sunlit snow. In a case like this, the meter reading would be greatly inflated by the snow, causing the figures to be under-exposed. In colour, this would mean the figures would come out far too dark, and the colours too dense for satisfactory projection or reproduction. The best method of correcting the exposure, of course, would be to approach the skiers and take a reading when their figures filled the frame, fix the exposure, then go back to the taking position. Of course, your footprints in the snow would probably ruin the composition! An easy way to correct would be to

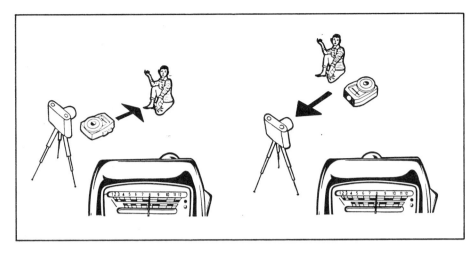

aim the camera up to the deep blue sky, which we want to come out that way, and take the reading from this. Another accurate method is known as the substitute reading. Here, you simply take the reading from your own hand, moving the camera close enough to fill the frame with it. It doesn't matter if the hand is out-of-focus, as this will not affect the reading.

These two situations, light against dark, and dark against light, are typical of non-average lighting situations, where

the meter, left to its own devices, would fail. In the light against dark situation it would cause over-exposure, and in the dark against light situation, under-exposure. It is sometimes difficult for the beginner to grasp the concept. In the case of skiers on the sunlit slope his first reaction would be, "This is very bright, and needs a shorter exposure". In fact, the opposite is the case. The illustrations on pages 50–57 demonstrate the principles of exposure correction.

This is an 'average' subject, where light, dark and mid-toned area are evenly distributed.

Thistles against a sunset sky were photographed through a 135mm lens. Exposure was keyed to the sky, silhouetting the thistles. Extra exposure to put detail in the thistles would have ruined the effect of silhouette and lightened the sky too much.

With the light becoming progressively less from left to right, exposure was keyed to the centre part of this beautiful room at Ballyseede Castle, Ireland. See opposite page, top. The camera was fitted with a 28mm lens, and Agfachrome 50S exposed at ⅛sec at f/5.6, using a tripod.

We are often told to give extra exposure for backlit subjects, but TTL-metering cameras usually work out the right exposure for themselves. The unmodified exposure, opposite page bottom, and the backlit effect is nicely retained. Famous gardener Percy Thrower teaches an assistant.

Incident light

When the meter, or metering camera, is pointed at the subject, it measures the various brightnesses reflected from the various surfaces, and integrates them. This is known as reflected light metering and, as we have seen, in a small number of non-average situations it is prone to error. There is another exposure method, considered by many professionals to be more consistently accurate, and known as the incident light method. It is usually confined to a separate, hand-held meter, though one or two cameras with built-in meters also have an incident light attachment. See diagram, page 49.

An incident light meter has a white plastic, translucent screen, often in the form of a hemisphere, covering the meter cell. Instead of being aimed at the subject, the meter is turned and aimed (usually from the subject position) towards the camera. Thus, it measures the light falling on the subject (incident light), not the light reflected from it. Incident light meters are calibrated always to give the correct exposure for skin tones, which, in colour photography, are the

one thing that must always be accurately exposed. In the case of our girl against a dark wall of foliage, or our skiers on a sunlit slope, the incident light meter would automatically give correct exposure for the part of the subject that matters, and the same applies to those ninety-five per cent of other situations we call average.

If incident light exposure is so accurate, why is the reflected light method so universally popular?

In the first place, it isn't possible to take an incident light reading through the pentaprism of an SLR, which is how most through-the-lens metering SLRs work. Second, aiming the metering camera at the subject is quicker, and permits the reading to be held right up to the moment of exposure, which may be critical when the light is constantly changing, as when clouds are flitting across the sun. Third, most manufacturers of metering cameras weigh up the fact that only five per cent of lighting situations are non-average, and that most photographers soon learn how to correct them.

Expert photographers are quite

happy, therefore, to use the reflected light system, even though they know that in a very few cases the incident light meter could be more accurate than the corrective judgments they make. When in doubt, an experienced colour photographer will bridge his exposures. That is, take one exposure at the indicated reading, two more at half and one stop less exposure, and two at half and one stop more. From these, one is bound to be correct.

Grey card method

For extreme accuracy in awkward lighting situations, the photographer can use the grey card method of exposure determination, which is particularly useful when copying documents or any flat artwork such as drawings or paintings. A grey card is just that. Kodak Limited can supply a packet of Kodak Neutral Test Cards, size 10 × 8in. The grey side has 18 per cent reflectance, while the white side will reflect 90 per cent of the light falling on it. In use, the grey card is held in the subject position, and the meter aimed at it. The meter has to be brought close enough for the card to fill the frame,

and care must be taken that the meter's shadow does not fall on the card.

The reading should be the same as that obtained with an incident light meter. The advantage is that the card itself is integrating the light, and the meter cannot be fooled by the different degrees of reflectance from various parts of the subject itself.

Flat artwork is particularly prone to exposure error when the reflected light method is used. The total area covered by the coloured lines on a drawing may be only two or three per cent of the white paper area. Similarly, white lines on a dark surface, as in a scraperboard drawing or blueprint. By placing a grey card over the artwork, TTL-metering, or any reflected light meter, is far more reliable.

Controls

Most cameras incorporate some means of overriding the automatic exposure, and the various mechanisms are described in Chapters Two and Four. Here, we can touch upon their use in correcting meter readings for non-average subjects. In the case of our skiers against the

The bright area by the window would cause under-exposure at the right. Exposure should be keyed to a middle-toned area, as indicated by the arrow.

In a view like this, the meter would give a high reading, and cause under-exposure of the snow, which would come out grey. An extra stop exposure should be given.

sunlit snow, it was suggested that the reading could be taken from the deep blue sky, and that this would also be correct for the skiers themselves. Most compact cameras, and quite a few SLRs, incorporate a 'memory hold'. The meter automatically sets the exposure, and this exposure is locked by taking the first pressure on the release button. In the example given, we would first aim the camera at the sky, take the first pressure on the release button, hold it there while re-composing the view, then take the second pressure to make the exposure. In the case of, say, a bright sky causing under-exposure to the foreground, we could dip the camera to include less of the sky, take the first pressure, re-compose, then expose.

With non-automatic cameras of the type known as match-needle, a manual needle or claw is centred on the meter

This subject looks contrasty, but the bright highlights balance the shadows. Just follow the meter indication.

As stained glass windows are illuminated by transmitted light, an incident reading cannot be taken. From the viewpoint shown, the dark walls and lead strips between the panes would cause over-exposure. To correct this, take the TTL-metering camera, or hand-held reflected light meter, close up to determine the exposure. Also, see Page Fifty-eight.

needle, by adjusting the aperture or shutter speed, or both. Once set, the exposure will not alter. Thus, there is no need to 'hold' the exposure while re-composing.

A certain kind of compact is of the fully automatic type, which has no facility for manual override. The exposure can still be adjusted, however, simply by altering the ASA setting. Therefore, to obtain one-third or two-thirds less exposure when using a 64 ASA film, set the ASA control to 80 or 100 ASA. You can go either side of this range in $\frac{1}{3}$rd stop increments: 25-32-40-50-64-80-100-125-160-200-250-320-400.

Note that there is still some tone on the sky. Using fast film in brightly-lit streets at dusk, the small amount of daylight present helps fill-in the shadows without spoiling the night effect, and fast exposures can be given. This was taken on Tri-X at 1/60sec at f/2.8 with a 35mm lens.

Some SLR cameras do not have the memory hold described above. Instead, they incorporate an exposure factor dial (internally linked to the ASA setting) by means of which as much as -2 to $+2$ stops variation may be set, in $\frac{1}{2}$ stop units. This is satisfactory for most purposes, but there are two disadvantages. First, the control is not infinitely variable, as with a memory hold on the release button. Second, it is all too easy to forget to cancel the exposure factor after use. It is quite easy to under- or over-expose the next few frames, or indeed the remainder of the film, before remembering. Even experienced professionals occasionally fall into this trap, especially when attention is concentrated on the subject. If you have this kind of camera, get into the habit of remembering!

Not too technical

When the beginner buys his first metering camera, or separate exposure meter, he expects the meter to be dead accurate. The advanced worker knows better. Because of the vagaries of electrical systems, and the impossibility of manufacturing light-sensitive cells with identically repeatable response, manufacturers regard $\frac{1}{3}$ stop error as an acceptable tolerance. In the majority of cases, meter response error is not equal over the whole brightness range. It may be accurate at high and medium light levels, but $\frac{1}{3}$ stop out in dim light, or *vice versa*. $\frac{1}{3}$ stop error is not critical, even with slide film.

It should also be remembered that different batches of film can vary slightly from the marked ASA rating, and actual shutter speeds may deviate a little from the marked ones. Happily, in the majority of situations, all these errors tend to cancel each other out. Very seldom will the metering or shutter speeds of a modern camera be seriously at fault, but if they are the instrument should be returned for servicing.

Attaining perfection in exposure under all circumstances depends on two things. First, what the individual photographer accepts as perfect, and second, experience backed up by evaluation. This is why, in your early days at least, make a note each time you decide to deviate from normal exposure. When it comes to examining your slides or negatives, this information will help you decide whether or not you did the right thing. Remember, most of the time the meter will give the right exposure even though it can't think.

58

6.
Composition

Composition is a feeling. A feeling for balance and rightness. The so-called rules of composition can help the beginner to avoid pitfalls, and to know what to look for, but in the end it comes down to maturity of vision. Not every photographer is cut out to be a great artist, but by diligent appraisal of the world around us we can arrive at critical vision. Our pictures will then take on that feeling of rightness which we call good composition. This sense of balance is not so difficult to achieve as the beginner may imagine, and this chapter is devoted to the methods and exercises by which he can instruct himself.

Building blocks

Put two photographers in front of a picturesque cottage–or a pair of old boots, for that matter–and one will produce a picture, while the other will produce a photograph. The former photographer is using his technique to produce a creative image, while the latter is simply aiming his camera and exercising his technique. There's a world of difference in the two approaches. Creative photography, and record photography.

To make the jump from one to the other, we need to change our attitude to the subject in front of us. We must start by pre-visualising just how we want the subject to appear on the finished slide or print, then use our technique to produce the desired effect. All too often, a photographer considers the subject too little, his mind taken up with the purely mechanical considerations of depth-of-field and exposure. To understand this

Here, the shutter speed has been set at $\frac{1}{4}$sec and the camera swung to keep the motorcyclist in the centre of the frame.

Although the window was photographed with a standard 50mm lens, a telephoto was used to determine the exposure. The TTL reading was thus confined to a few panes of glass, and was uninfluenced by the dark surroundings. The 50mm lens was then replaced for the exposure. See also Page Fifty-six.

more fully, we must appreciate the nature of the photographic image. A useful start is to consider the difference between the mediums used by the painter and the photographer; and, their similarities.

The painter builds up his image on the canvas by applying paint. The photographer captures it instantaneously by photo-chemical means. The painter can use drawing to alter the relationship between objects, and can leave things out. The photographer alters relationships by choice of viewpoint and choice of focal length. This is also his only means of leaving things out. The painter can intensify, reduce and even alter colours and shadows at will. The photographer

(c) Taken with a 16mm lens within a couple of feet of the arch. The arch seems to soar and sufficient detail of the ruins can be seen beyond. The effect is more pictorially interesting.

long shadows, helpful in building up a composition. At noon, it stands high in the sky. Shadows are small. The landscape looks flatter and the hills have less modelling. In outdoor portraits, dark, vertical shadows fill the eye sockets and the areas below nose and chin. Dramatic or pictorial backlighting is not possible, because the sun is overhead. In the shade things are different. Depending on the sun and the reflective surfaces around the subject area, the quality of light will change. It may be dull and sombre, or bright, suggesting the glare beyond the shade. We must train our eyes to appreciate every subtle or strong lighting effect in terms of pictorial value.

Colour

A common mistake made by the beginner, is to go in search of brilliant and variegated colours. It is as though he were determined to get the utmost value from his colour film, cramming every frame with as much colour as can be packed in. Strong colour suggests brightness, vivacity, vibrant life, and can be used to portray these qualities. But it can also destroy a sense of delicacy, gentleness, subtlety, which are best suggested with muted or pastel colours.

We should start by realising that the strength of colour is controlled by the light falling on the coloured surface. The brighter the light, the brighter the colour. Towards twilight colours become muted, and in the dark there are no colours at all. Thus, in the pictorial sense, light gives us considerable control over colour.

Next, we must recognise the psychological effect of various colours. Red is the colour of fire, Man's primeval enemy. Just a small amount of red goes a long way in a picture. Blue and green, on the other hand, are the colours of sky and grass. They soothe the eye, even when present in large areas. The 'classic' landscape has a large expanse of green and blue, with one small figure dressed in red. A small area of red balances a large area of green or blue. It is often said that warm colours belong in the foreground, while cool colours are best used in the background. A common mistake made by the beginner, is to seat a model in front of a red curtain. If the model is dressed in blue, it often looks as though the model is being seen through a cutout in the curtain. The red has advanced, the blue receded.

These are guidelines, not rules. They

achieves similar results by using filters and choosing the right time of day. Both painter and photographer are creating the illusion of three-dimensional images on a flat surface, and usually within the bounds of a rectangle.

Study any photograph and you see that it is made up of shapes, lines and masses, contrasting in varying degrees. By means of his technique, the photographer can control this image strongly and effectively. The building blocks at his disposal are light, colour, contrast, and blur. We can study these one at a time, and see how they add up.

Light

The first thing we have to do is consider light in terms of its quality, not its quantity. Is it harsh, pearly, soft? Not how fast a shutter speed it will allow. Morning and evening the sun is low and casts

A 16mm lens, not corrected for linear distortion, enabled the archway and gate to be photographed very close. The curvature adds to the compositional effect.

do not mean that large areas of red must never be included, nor that green or blue must always be in large areas. Lots of red can be used to suggest excitement or danger. A small figure in a green dress will accentuate the brilliance of a field of poppies.

Now we come to the question of complementary colours. As you certainly know, a complementary is opposed to a primary colour.

primary	complementary
red	green
yellow	brown
blue	orange

Each complementary is composed of the other two primaries. It is so-called simply because it complements the opposite colour. You can obtain a colour wheel from any art shop, and the rela-

tionships between primary, complementary and tertiary colours can be instantly seen. This is a useful exercise, but again, there are no rigid principles that must be adhered to. It boils down to appreciation and taste, which come with observation and experience.

Contrast

In general, a few bold shapes arranged to offset and complement each other, make a more effective composition (are more satisfying to the eye) than a mass of detail. Make no mistake about it, Nature knows nothing about composition, but everything about form. Nature never puts a rectangular frame round its creations. Only Man does that. We can observe frameless Nature with our eyes, permitting our gaze to rove from hill to tree, from stream to rocky outcrop. We may recognise that a certain configuration of a windswept tree on a hillside has 'possibilities', but only when we begin to frame the subject in the viewfinder are we faced with the need to compose within the frame. We have to consider the various elements of the subject, those building bricks, and arrange them in a satisfying, significant, or meaningful way within the rectangle. The illustrations on pages 59–88, demonstrate how this balance can be achieved.

Blur

Motion in a picture can be suggested by a degree of blur, which we obtain by using a slow shutter speed, or moving the camera during exposure, or both. If we photograph a racing car at a very high shutter speed, we will freeze both car and background. The impression of speed is lost, and we might just as well have photographed a stationary car. If, on the other hand, we choose a shutter speed of around 1/250sec, and swing the camera so that the moving car is still in

A 21mm wideangle was used for this bleak shot. The extreme perspective and contrasty printing help to give mood.

A 16mm lens emphasises the shapes of this old corner of Shrewsbury, England. Note the size of the nearest cobblestones.

the centre of the viewfinder, the car will be sharp and the background will have lateral blur, which suggests speed.

The same applies to moving water. Photograph it at too high a shutter speed, and the movement is lost. 1/60sec will give a sharp enough image, but not enough to freeze the movement. If the camera is mounted on a tripod, a very slow shutter speed, between $\frac{1}{4}$-1 sec may be used. River bank, grasses and background will remain sharp, while the water will extend in foamy coils, creating

a powerful sense of movement.

Naturally, where the beauty or significance of a scene depends on the rendering of fine detail, we want as much sharpness as possible, and this is an area where the incredible recording ability of the lens comes into its own. At the same time, we must recognise that extreme sharpness is not to be sought with every subject. Sharpness, or the lack of it, is one of the photographic tools at our disposal, with which we can suggest any degree of stillness or movement.

Choice of focal length is a valuable compositional tool. The picture above, left, was taken with an 85mm lens, that on the right with a 200mm lens from a greater distance, while the shot, below, right, was taken with a 21mm wideangle.

Reflections give you twice the picture, but can combine to make a single composition. Both these pictures were taken in Ireland with a small compact camera.

66

7.
Pictorial Photography

In the last chapter we dealt with composition, and how to arrange the various elements of a subject to form a satisfying picture within the frame. Now we must consider a word which is often used by serious amateurs, to describe the kind of photography that most camera clubs are concerned with. The word is pictorial. Camera clubs usually divide their competition work into categories, such as portrait, colour (as though this were a subject on its own), photo-journalism, and pictorial. To be suitable for this last category, a picture has to be arranged according to the guidelines suggested in the last chapter, usually with a good balance of shapes and mass,

A black line can be drawn round a picture to 'contain' it, when marginal areas are white.

with the main subject matter well within the frame, and no lines leading the eye towards the margins. Pictorial, more often than not, simply means well composed. And yet, in club photography, however well composed a sports shot or portrait may be, it does not fall into the pictorial category. In fact, what most clubs mean by the word pictorial, is simply landscapes or views.

Competitions

A great many amateurs do very well with submissions to club and photo magazine competitions, especially in the pictorial section. This is only partly because

The detail in the sun-splashed areas could have been retained by printing on a soft grade of paper. However, the contrast was preferred, as this accentuates the man and his donkey.

This peaceful scene was taken through a green filter, which helps differentiate the various greens of foliage.

landscape subjects are readily available to the amateur, and do not require special facilities such as press passes or a fully equipped studio. In fact, where pictorial work is concerned, the amateur is at no disadvantage *vis à vis* the professional. Because the amateur has more time to devote to pictorialism, which is not a highly paid genre, his work is often better. If you feel that your pictures are good enough for entry in a particular competition, go right ahead and submit. Too many photographers moan that 'the same old names' keep appearing among the lists of winners, and use this as an excuse for not submitting their own work. If you never try, you never win. Your work may be as good, or even better, than the pictures you constantly see hung on club walls, or printed in photo magazines, the difference being that those 'same old names' go to the trouble of submitting their pictures.

The prizes that can be won in competitions organised by photo magazines are well worth the effort of entering. Excellent cameras are usually offered as first prize, followed by many useful items of equipment. Manufacturers of photo-

graphic products also organise competitions through the pages of photo magazines. These sometimes offer equipment as prizes, though prize money is also offered, and this may run to a thousand pounds or more.

Competitions in photo magazines almost always have sensible rules, the most important being that (a) copyright remains with the photographer, and (b) that the prize will be considered full payment for reproduction. Reproduction is usually confined to printing the winning pictures, and possible use for publicity purposes connected with the competitions. In the case of those competitions organised by manufacturers, for example, copies of the prize-winning pictures are sent to all photo magazines for free reproduction. Those manufacturers with a really ethical approach to competitions, also offer a bonus payment if a certain picture is later chosen for advertising purposes.

What you have to be careful of, is such sweeping statements as: all pictures submitted become the copyright of the organisers, and may be used by them for whatever purpose. Rules like this will

this is a ready market for the amateur. It will never make you rich, but by carefully studying the preferences of each magazine, it is possible to pay for your hobby and even make a little extra.

For colour covers, most national magazines will consider nothing smaller than a 6×6cm transparency, though photo magazines will often use a really good 35mm slide. Do study the cover layout of each magazine. Some have the title (logo) actually printed on the upper part of the picture, which means that you have to leave sufficient space at the top of the frame to accommodate the title. If you don't, your picture cannot be used, however much the editor may like it.

A decision that always has to be made—upright or horizontal format? Your decision should be based on which can best concentrate all the important subject matter within the frame.

mainly be found in competitions organised by firms producing non-photographic products. More often than not, the organisers simply do not understand the unethical implications of the wording, or have copied the rules from some other competition. Others certainly look upon a competition as a cheap way of providing themselves with good publicity and advertising pictures. Read the small print!

The pictorial market

Apart from the photo magazines, there are many other markets for pictorial work. Country Life, The Field, and any number of magazines devoted to country topics, are always needing good colour covers and black & white pictures, and

Remember, too, that most magazines require an upright picture for the cover, or for an inside page devoted to pictorial work. A horizontal shot cannot occupy more than half a page.

Market study is a sonorous phrase, but it simply means studying magazines to analyse their requirements. You would be surprised how many people submit colour slides to newspapers which do not print colour, or send pictures which are of interest to a specialist market to a general-interest magazine.

Amateurs often talk about submitting pictures to firms which produce calendars, but have only a hazy idea of the requirement. They simply hope that a particular firm may take a liking to a picture, and find a place for it. In fact, the amateur who can produce fine pictorial transparencies has quite a wide market open to him. The Writers' and Artists' Yearbook lists well over twenty firms which consider pictures for calendars, posters and greetings cards of various kinds. Most of these firms prefer large transparencies, and some even stipulate 'no 35mm'.

With more and more concrete being poured over the landscape, there is a nostalgia for the peaceful country view, traditional crafts, old inn signs, thatched cottages, country characters and so on, and this is where the amateur can score.

Don't scorn the corn

The idea of the traditional postcard picture, which used to be scorned by pictorialists, is changing. Professionals who specialise in viewcards will often spend whole days at a particular location, probably a noted beauty spot or village, just waiting for a perfect lighting effect. Gone are the days when a snap was taken in black & white, and then laboriously coloured, with cottonwool puffs of cloud. Today, the viewcard public wants something better.

If the amateur devotes himself only to well-known beauty spots, which have been photographed many thousands of times, he is seriously limiting his chances of success. He would do far better to hunt out attractive pictures in less frequented areas. Here is an example from my own experience. I once visited a village

Stonehenge, England. The sky was darkened with an orange filter. The sun was allowed to influence the exposure, ensuring a dark sky and silhouette. The lens was stopped down to f/16, which will usually ensure the star effect without a special attachment being used. Simple contrast, the high sun, and relatively small area of the ancient monument, suggests remoteness.

More space has been left in front of the rider than behind. He is thus travelling 'into' the frame, instead of out of it.

notable for its beauty, which had attracted many professional viewcard photographers over the years. Nearly all produced the same view, showing part of the main street, including the four most attractive houses. At the end of the street could be seen the village pump, but not one photographer had thought it worthwhile to do a close-up. While I was studying the pump, two sun-bronzed young people came down the street. The man and the girl were both in shorts, both very attractive, and both had bright orange backpacks. After a chat, they were persuaded to sit on the low wall surrounding the pump, while a picture was taken. They were promised, and later received, a couple of colour prints made from the best slide. This picture was printed several times in photo magazines, and, through an agent, was later sold to a viewcard company and sold in tens of thousands to holidaymakers.

It is certainly not worthwhile to hunt pictorial subjects with the sole aim of viewcard or greeting card use. The approach should be much more general, with the prime aim to produce a good picture that will serve many purposes, not least of which is your own satisfaction. Where possible, take both upright and

horizontal shots, and take more than one of each. This means that an original slide can be submitted to more than one market at a time. In this respect, make sure you do not submit the same picture to two *competing* markets. For example, an ordinary pictorial view could be submitted to any number of magazines on a non-exclusive basis, but a picture with topical interest must never be submitted as an exclusive to two newspapers at the same time. It is also unlikely that a viewcard company would object to a secondary sale made to a magazine, or *vice versa*.

One of the corniest, and most successful, pictures I ever took, was of a tabby cat sitting on the wall of a churchyard at sunset. The exposure was kept short to darken the rather pale colours in the sky, the church tower itself was almost silhouetted, and a small flash unit with a handkerchief draped over the front provided enough fill-in to fully illuminate the cat. At the crucial moment a helper dabbed a trace of fish paste on the cat's nose, and in the picture he is licking his lips ecstatically.

It is worth remembering that unlike dedicated pictorialists, the average member of the public (who buys viewcards) does not appreciate a rather

The old, deserted house in Shropshire, England, was rather bleak when standing alone. A 28mm lens was used to get the flowers close up in the foreground.

A really powerful sky is effective, even without a particularly interesting foreground. A red filter was used for contrast.

The entire frame is not much more than a snapshot, but the black line shows the area selected for enlargement, providing a much stronger composition.

The rule of thirds is a good guide to composition. Important subject matter should be on one of the points E, G, F, H. A strong object at F can be balanced by a minor one at G, and so on. Horizon lines are best at A or B, not cutting the picture into two equal rectangles. Lines C and D are equivalent to horizon lines in some vertical compositions. Subject matter should be directed towards the centre of the frame. Important subject matter should be kept away from the margins.

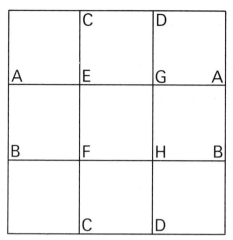

Composition is a feeling. Although the lone sheep is walking towards a corner of the frame in contravention of the rule of thirds it is well balanced by the farm and the clump of trees at the left.

abstract picture of paint peeling from an old wall. The card he or she sends home should show clearly a view of the vacation spot, or local activity. A picture of a local potter at his wheel may be best for a photo magazine or a camera club competition, but for a viewcard it might be best to take a close-up of him outdoors, holding a couple of pots, against a background of the pottery and village street. Even though this is a posed record, it can still be handled pictorially, and will have a far greater appeal.

Club competitions

Tens of thousands of amateurs benefit by joining a local camera club. Membership is invaluable to the beginner, who, benefitting from advice given by more advanced members, can learn much and avoid many expensive errors. Camera clubs, or photographic societies, usually meet one evening a week, and provide both social and photographic activities. There are lectures, slide talks and demonstrations, and very often a darkroom is

provided for the use of members. A few of the more important clubs also have a studio equipped with various forms of lighting and rolls of background paper.

Considering the benefits, membership fees are very low, just a few pounds a year, and husband-and-wife memberships cost relatively less. If you do not know of a local camera club, the information is always obtainable by telephoning the town hall or the local newspaper office.

Club competitions are often divided into categories for beginners, intermediate and advanced workers. Entry into the last two categories often depends on success in the first. 'Print' and 'Slide' competitions are usually on a monthly and quarterly basis, with the yearly competition culminating in an exhibition to which the public is invited. Naturally, there is a strong competitive element among club members, but this hardly ever interferes with the general sense of camaraderie and helpfulness.

Judging is usually carried out by an invited judge, normally a distinguished photographer from the club 'circuit', whose knowledge qualifies him for this exacting task. The beginner would do well to recognise the fact that there are no norms or absolutes in judging—marks will always depend on the taste of the individual judge. Fortunately, club judges are, on the whole, very good at their job, and few complaints are heard. When they are, the judge in question

The 'story' of a subject cannot always be told in a single picture. Alone, the general view of the inn would not be very interesting, but note the message just inside the doorway.

This was taken with a tube of coloured cellophane held in front of the lens. Try scraps of coloured paper round a clear acetate tube, or shoot through a hole in coloured cellophane. The effects you can obtain in this way are unending.

isn't invited to make a further visit. There is an old saying in club circles, that the good judge is the one who gives you the prize! Whether or not every member present agrees with a particular judgment, there is no doubt that a great deal can be learned by listening to the analyses of pictures by a competent judge.

It has often been argued that club competitions can stifle individuality and creativeness, as the entrants set out to please the judge rather than themselves. There is a story about two members discussing the judge for a forthcoming competition. ''Old Jackson,'' said one, ''is a sucker for oily reflections in water—we'd better dig out some of our oily reflection negatives.'' In fact, the average member stands to learn a great deal from the comments of judges, even when he has not personally entered any pictures.

8.
Portraits, Outdoors And In

There are two basic kinds of portraiture, formal and informal. In formal portraiture, taken in a studio, backgrounds, lighting effects and poses are carefully arranged and studied until, in the eyes of the photographer, a pleasing study has been composed. Informal portraiture, often taken outdoors, permits the photographer to work faster, and is more likely to capture an aspect of personality. This may suggest that less attention is paid to lighting, backgrounds and poses, but this is not necessarily the case.

How the individual photographer approaches portraiture will depend on his attitude to technique, as well as to people. Some camera owners get a great deal of pleasure from arranging lighting equipment, are always striving for technical perfection, and incline towards the formal approach. For others, the camera is simply a means by which they can capture the fleeting expressions and other glimpses of personality which intrigue them. Whichever approach attracts each photographer, there is a world of difference between portraits taken to please the sitter, and those taken to please the photographer. A character study of an elderly person, with every

A Cockney Pearly Queen, with every button pin sharp. Taken under a hazy sun, all the shadows are nicely filled in. Agfachrome 50S, with an 85mm lens on a Rolleiflex SL35E. Exposure was about 1/250sec at f/5.6.

A candid shot in which the workman is looking out of the frame but well balanced by the trowel. This kind of compositional rule-breaking pays dividends once you develop a sense of balance.

crowsfoot and line of experience sharply delineated, may please the photographer but horrify the sitter.

The formal approach

Many years ago, portraitists were formal simply because slow exposures were needed and the sitter just had to sit still. Early commercial studios had either huge windows and skylights, like the studios of painters, or, later, were filled with banks of lights to provide a high enough level of lighting. With the advent of proper studio lighting, the five-light set-up became increasingly popular. The most important lamp was the modeller, usually a powerful bulb in a dish reflector, giving directional light with diffused edges to the shadows. This was normally placed about 45° to one side of the camera, and 45° high. Next came the fill-in. This was a smaller lamp in an ordinary reflector, which had the job of relieving the heavy shadows. It was placed as close as possible to the camera, to avoid casting secondary shadows. The third lamp was called a separation lamp. Placed behind the sitter, it illuminated the background. Its purpose was to control the tone of the background and remove any shadows cast by the modeller or fill-in lamps. It had the effect of 'separating' the sitter from the background. Finally, there were two effect lights, usually placed on either side and well to the rear of the sitter. They provided highlights on the hair, cheek, neck, and clothing.

The separation and effect lights were usually in the form of spotlights, the diameter of the spot being controllable. They became popular not only with formal portraitists, but also with the glamour photographers of Hollywood, and subsequently the world. This form of lighting is still used by a few portrait specialists, but has given way in popularity to a more diffused form of illumination.

As far as the amateur is concerned, the main drawback to formal portraiture is the need for more space than is available in the average house. Even for a half-length, separation and effect lights cannot be fully exploited unless there is a distance of six to nine feet behind the sitter, and twice this in the case of a full-length. Sitter-camera distance can also be a problem indoors, not to mention the space needed for the modeller and fill-in lights.

For these reasons, the amateur often confines himself to working with just one or two lamps, the most useful being the modeller in a large dish reflector, and a fill-in in a smaller reflector. Useful lamps are 500w for the modeller, 200w for the fill-in. In most cases, the sitter is too close to the background, with no feeling of separation. It is this, rather than technical expertise, which so often distinguishes the work of the amateur from that of the professional.

The old lady in Crete was aware that she was being photographed, but as the camera was at a distance with a 200mm lens, she did not feel intruded upon.

Artist Lawrence Klonaris at work on a painting. This was taken by daylight in his studio, with the camera on a tripod. Exposure was 1/30sec at f/5.6 with 50 ASA Agfachrome film.

The best approach

If he has sufficient space, the amateur can use a single lamp to combine the purposes of the separation and effect lights. It can be arranged to one side, so that most of its light falls on the background, with a little spilling over on to the sitter. A modeller and fill-in remain essential. Some amateurs content themselves with the use of a single umbrella flash, described in Chapter Thirteen. This is certainly convenient, as it stops all the action, thus permitting hand-held exposures, but the unrelieved back-ground often causes a dull effect. Also unless the umbrella flash incorporates a tungsten modelling lamp, it is not possible to judge the lighting effect in advance. Nevertheless, the umbrella flash provides the amateur with portrait lighting capable of good results, and can easily be stowed away.

Informal indoors

Excellent portraits can be taken indoors by daylight, with no form of supplementary lighting other than a white towel or a sheet of white card to act as a reflector.

Using a large aperture gives limited depth of field, especially in close-ups. With the focus here sharply on the pot, the fact that the potter's face is out of focus is not important. In fact, it helps to emphasise the pot.

This Greek farmer was photographed against the light with a 105mm lens on an automatic camera. The centre-weighted metering has taken care of the skin tones without giving extra exposure.

The sitter is placed near a window, at an angle of 45–90°. The white towel or card is simply supported on a chair on the other side of the sitter, and brought close enough to lighten the shadows. A little experience is needed to judge the right amount of fill-in. If the reflector is brought too close it will swamp the shadows completely, and the portrait will lack model-ling. Taken too far away, the effect will be negligible. When starting, it is a good idea to take a number of trial portraits with the reflector at various distances, so that the results can be evaluated. This will be time well spent.

Daylight always look natural, and portraits taken in this way can be very powerful. One problem is that the wall behind the sitter is usually well in the shade, and in a black & white photograph may merge into the hair of a dark-haired sitter. This can often be corrected by aiming a lamp at the background, or even by switching on a desk or standard lamp. Provided none of this tungsten illumination reaches the front of the sitter, the effect can be most attractive even on daylight type colour film. Of course, with a blonde sitter, the dark background will matter far less.

When taking head-and-shoulder portraits near a window, an ordinary home projection screen forms an excellent plain background. Its tone can be darkened from white through progressive shades of grey, by moving it back from the direct window light.

In larger rooms, especially when the rest of the family take an indulgent view of his hobby, the photographer can set up a pair of Vendorpoles with one or two rolls of background paper, in a

Almost a good composition, but spoiled by the lower fence log. Mask this off just below the elbow, and see how the picture is strengthened.

The dark surroundings would
have caused over-exposure in
this shot of a guardsman.
Either take the reading very
close and then return to the
taking position, or use an
incident light meter, which will
not be affected by the
surroundings.

Three ways to treat an indoor subject by daylight. In the top left picture, soft daylight from the side gives good modelling to the figure. In the top, right picture a splash of colour is added by the red shirt. For the bottom picture, a pale magenta colour printing filter was placed over the lens.

semi-permanent position along one wall. The paper can be rolled down and across the floor to provide a seamless background. For black & white work, rolls of white, black, and a mid-toned paper of any colour will do. Black is also useful in colour work, but where coloured paper is concerned, the beginner is advised to start with the lighter shades, as it is surprising how these darken in the picture. This is because the light reaching the background is usually weaker than that reaching the sitter. Pale blue in preference to dark blue, and so on. Probably the most useful background colours for portraiture are light blue and light brown. The former is particularly effective in setting off brightly-coloured clothing, and the latter provides an excellent complement to skin tones. Yellow, and especially red, should be treated with care, and, although there are exceptions, green is best reserved for still life work, as it may introduce an unpleasant cast to skin colour.

Action lighting

In formal portraiture, a tripod and slow film are used, in order to obtain smooth, grainfree gradation of skin tones. At the

Cigarette smoker by window light. Note the psychological effect of the large shadow area. Careful use of space, and dimensional relationship of subject and background, are a powerful tool of composition.

same time, this limits the freedom of both photographer and model to move, which is why anything more active than a slow smile is difficult in formal work. That sudden command "Hold it!" can ruin any revelation of personality.

With action portraiture things are different. It is quite easy to set up brilliant indoor lighting, permitting fast hand-held exposures with medium-speed or fast film, both of which are obtainable in colour as well as black & white. In this more candid type of portraiture, we want to avoid those carefully arranged shadows associated with formal work. Diffused lighting gives adequate modelling, even though the sitter or photographer changes position.

Perhaps the ideal lighting for this kind of work, is a single lamp aimed at the ceiling, and there is no reason why this should not be flash. Bounce-flash technique is described fully in Chapter Thirteen. Apertures required are comparatively small, giving enough depth-of-field to cover small focusing errors or

sudden movements of the sitter towards or away from the camera, and the flash exposure ensures sharp images. However, a continuous light source has important advantages. The light is bright enough to make focusing easy, even when the subject is moving, and the lighting effect, especially as regards the sparkle in the eyes, can be observed all the time.

The least useful power for a lamp turned up towards the ceiling is 500w, and a lamp of the Argaphoto type is to be recommended. This has a colour temperature of 3200°K (see Chapter Five), which is balanced for use with Type B (or L) slide films. Most useful is Kodak Ektachrome 160, which has enough speed for the purpose. Even more useful is a ciné lamp with tungsten halogen tube, with an output of 1000w or more. Turned up to the ceiling of the average room, and used with Ektachrome 160 or medium-speed black & white film, exposures in the region of 1/125sec at f/2.8 are possible.

Outdoor portraits

The great outdoors provides the best studio anyone could wish for, with an infinite number of backgrounds and lighting effects. However, unless the photographer is blessed with a really spacious and landscaped garden, he is advised to take his sitter farther afield. Often, when taking a portrait in an ordinary garden, the position of the sun dictates the position of the sitter, and this usually means that a brick wall or some other unphotogenic object forms the background. Brick walls are a menace! The pattern of brickwork can seldom be eliminated, except when working with a telephoto lens at a wide aperture, and even then only in a close-up.

Somewhere within reach of your home is a park, the gardens of a stately home, an open space, or some attractive architecture, which is far more suitable for a portrait session. In most parks there is at least one area where an expanse of grass is backed by some dark trees, which form an attractive out-of-focus background. By posing the model either to left or right, a whole variety of lighting effects can be obtained. If the sun is really harsh, portraits can be taken under the shade of the trees. With the exposure set for the shaded sitter, the open area beyond the trees will then be

Some of the lighting equipment available for amateur use. The large dish reflector with inverted cup is ideal for modelling. The light is directional but with soft-edged shadows. The smaller reflectors are best for fill-in and effect lighting. The umbrella is often used alone, with flash, for general portrait lighting.

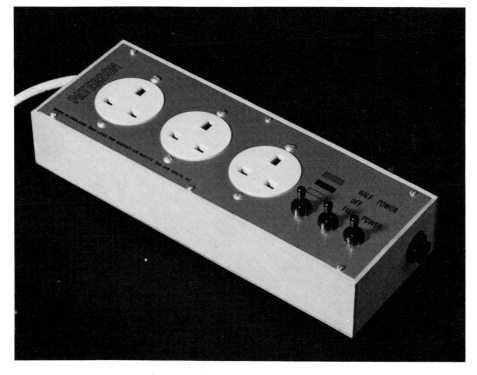

A useful junction box. Lamps may be used singly or in series at reduced or full power, and a tangle of wires is avoided.

These three portraits were taken with yellow, blue and magenta Centre-Spot filters. They have a clear centre spot, so only the surrounding area is coloured.

over-exposed, and form a bright background with irritating detail conveniently 'burnt out'.

Some parks have a bye-law forbidding the use of a tripod without prior permission, but there is usually no objection even to professional work, provided that the camera is hand-held. One famous London park, incidentally, still has a bye-law forbidding wheelchairs to be ridden three abreast! Weekdays, in the morning or afternoon, are the best time to choose for photography in parks, as there are fewer people about. Naturally, if your interests lie in nude work, the local park will provide too many distractions—for visitors and park keepers, as well as your model. Not to mention the police. Outside the big cities, there are always woods and country walks open to the public, and on weekdays many of these areas are deserted. Provided you and your model are discreet, and a dressing gown is carried, nude sessions can be uneventful and rewarding.

Posing

Too many beginners try to twist their sitters into unnatural and exotic poses, under the impression that a really relaxed portrait will be unremarkable, or simply because the photographer has no clear idea of what he is trying to achieve. In fact, an amateur sitter, of either sex, will never look really good when asked to twist into an unnatural posture. This, of course, does not mean that the sitter should always be facing the camera, with hands hanging at the sides, à la countless million snapshots.

In general, a head-and-shoulder portrait looks better if taken from an angle. Simply by having the sitter turn away slightly, then turn the head towards the lens, a more active and spontaneous effect is achieved. In a half-length, a similar twist of torso and head towards the camera is far better than the head-on effect. The same principle applies to the seated figure. A sitter with knees crossed, turning the upper half of the body towards the camera, looks relaxed, but provides a far more interesting pose.

Where arms or legs are extended towards the camera, it is best to work from a greater distance with a moderate telephoto lens. This will avoid exaggerated perspective. Unless for dramatic or humorous effects, this kind of pose should be avoided by the photographer

90

who is limited to a standard lens. Examples of good and bad posing should be collected. Any amateur who wants to go seriously into portraiture, would be well advised to clip from magazines any portrait or pose which he considers particularly effective. These can be photographed, and small prints made to fill the pages of a small autograph or notebook. By studying such pictures, the photographer will be able to analyse the conditions under which they were taken, and the instructions, if any, that were given to the model. It will be noticed that many of the most successful pictures are subtly posed, to emphasise good features, but without those exaggerated or contorted poses from which the beginner's portrait session tends to suffer. If a certain pose from the notebook is shown to an amateur sitter, he or she can grasp what is required far better than listening to a lengthy explanation.

Make-up

The big cosmetic manufacturers, such as Max Factor, provide ranges of make-up especially for photographic work, the colours being suitable for various types of lighting. The application of such make-up is an art which has to be learned. Cleansing of the skin, foundation, shadow, rouge, lip-lining, mascara, powdering over – these things can be learned in a three-day course, and there are books available where the various stages are shown.

The amateur photographer is well advised to let his female sitters apply their own make-up in their usual way, but avoiding such things as dark eye-liners, which may look good in the street, but look harsh and contrived in a picture. On the other hand, every amateur portraitist should buy a stick of Max Factor's Erace. This looks and handles something like a lipstick, but is whitish. Applied to pimples and other facial blemishes, then powdered over, it is the best skin treatment (photographically speaking) of all time. Finally, remember that a soft-focus attachment over the lens, also provides a useful substitute for a skin tonic, which is appreciated by many male as well as female sitters.

9.
Holiday Pictures

When preparing for a holiday, the most important thing to remember is that you will be away from your home base, which includes your regular photographic dealer. Spares and repairs, sometimes more difficult to obtain abroad, can make all the difference between photographic success and failure. In this chapter we shall go over the various points which the experienced traveller is careful to attend to.

Checklist

If you don't already have a checklist of equipment and materials, this should be prepared well in advance of your holiday. It's easy enough to jot down your camera, lenses and flash, but there are a number of small items which are easily forgotten. An adapter ring for fitting a screw-in lens to a bayonet camera mount is one such item. Small, and easily overlooked when packing, its omission could force you to take all your pictures on the standard lens. The same applies to things like a tripod bush adapter, which could prevent you mounting the camera on a tripod, an extension lead for your flashgun, or even the separate computer if your flash outfit has this facility. Many flashguns have sealed-in nicad batteries, and the charger is easily forgotten. It is also easy to forget to switch the charger voltage to suit the country you are travelling to. All these items should be noted in logical sequence on your checklist, and gone over item by item when packing.

What to take

The amateur photographer going on holiday often looks upon his trip as the photographic excursion of the year, during which he is going to replenish his stock of pictures for slide talks and competition entries for the coming year. It

seldom works out that way, simply because he forgets that the holiday is also for relaxation, and that those travelling with him don't want to spend their time trailing round after the photographer.

For the professional, or advanced amateur, humping around a weighty outfit of cameras, lenses and other equipment, may be a necessity or a pleasure, but the average amateur will find himself taking more pictures if he carries less. There comes a time when the shoulder-sag caused by a heavy gadget bag detracts from the enthusiasm of picture-seeking and picture-making. Let me give you an example. When I travel professionally, I carry two large aluminium cases of equipment, as well as a shoulder bag. One case contains my 645 camera with 50mm, 80mm and 150mm lenses, plus filters and Lunasix exposure meter. The other case contains a second 35mm SLR camera body, plus 16mm, 21mm, 35–105mm zoom, 200mm and 300mm lenses, a large selection of plain and special effects filters, and many small items. In the gadget bag I carry a 35mm SLR camera with 28mm, 50mm, 105mm and 135mm lenses, plus half a dozen filters.

The two large cases travel in the boot of the car, together with a tripod and a box of films. At the location, I change the contents of the gadget bag according to the type of photography I am undertaking for any particular session. My flash gear consists of two powerful one-piece flashguns, a Rollei 140RES and a bigger Rollei E36RE with separate computer, plus various leads and a slave unit. As these are only used for interior work at night (usually cabaret, folk sessions and so on) all the flash gear is stowed in a separate bag, also carried in the car. I make it a rule to keep everything in the boot, never inside the car where it can be seen by passers-by. In some countries this is

an open invitation to not-so-petty crooks who specialise in break-and-entry thefts from tourists' cars. Even with these commonsense precautions, make sure before you leave that your equipment insurance covers the period of travel.

The point is, with a small gadget bag over my shoulder I don't notice the weight, so my concentration is not distracted from the surroundings, which is where the pictures lie.

Many photographers take both black & white and colour, and carry two cameras, each loaded with one type of film. It sounds an ideal arrangement, if you can afford it, but there are certain drawbacks. In the first place, colour and black & white photography call for two entirely different ways of seeing. If the significance or beauty of the subject depends on form, black & white may be the ideal medium, and occasionally the addition of colour may even detract from the effect. If the attraction of the subject is largely in its coloration, then obviously colour film is the best choice. However, it is almost impossible, even for the expert, to

Where the sun is harsh, either use a trace of flash fill-in, as here, or place a white towel as a reflector on the ground in front of the model. Often, there is sufficient reflection from the sand. A 6x6cm shot on Kodak Ektachrome film.

Pictures on the beach are often spoiled by people in the background, or confusing detail. Here, the location was carefully chosen, and appears isolated, though many people were nearby. This was a 6x6cm shot on Kodak Ektachrome film.

A low angle has also lowered the horizon, making the blue sky act as background. A twin-lens Rolleiflex shot on Kodak Ektachrome film.

Don't be afraid of backlighting, which can produce excellent modelling, but make sure the shadow areas have sufficient exposure. Half a stop is usually enough, as more will wash out the skin colour. A telephoto has put the background out of focus, even though a fairly small aperture was used. Kodak Ektachrome film.

switch his thinking from colour to black & white, and back again. One moment you are trying to think in terms of black, white and grey, the next in colour.

Because of this, many creative professionals prefer to work with only one type of film at a time, perhaps for a whole day. With the camera loaded with colour, you may miss a few good black & white shots, but your colour work is likely to be more effective, and *vice versa*. That's the way I prefer to work on holiday, with the emphasis on colour slides. Later, if necessary, I can get colour or black & white prints from my slides. Another advantage, is that I don't have the weight and inconvenience of working with, and carrying, two cameras at one time, and have only one film speed to bear in mind.

Many experienced photographers go on holiday with just a compact 35mm camera, or a 645 SLR camera, each of which is an outfit in itself. With a small flashgun and a couple of filters carried in the pocket, there is less thought of equipment, and a surprising number of good pictures are the result – with a more relaxing holiday, too.

Carrying film

If you live in Britain or the United States, buy all the film you need before leaving. In most of Europe film prices are about the same, but in the Middle and Far East they can be exorbitant. A roll of Kodachrome costs twice as much in India as in Europe. Obviously, you will have studied holiday brochures, and in some countries, you will notice, there is a limit to how many unexposed films you can bring in with you. In practice, you will find that such regulations are seldom enforced. Nevertheless, if you do have a hundred rolls of film with you, it could be advisable to let a companion carry half of them.

Another reason for buying your film before you leave, is that your favourite may not be easily obtained abroad, though nowadays Kodak and Agfa stock are found universally. Even when you do find what you want, the only available stock may be fast approaching the expiry date on the carton. You can use film months, or even years, past the expiry date if it has spent most of its life under refrigeration or in a cool climate, but on a dealer's shelf in a hot country, the film you buy needs to be as fresh as possible. Buying at home, you can ensure that you are carrying only fresh stock. It is advisable to look at the cartons, and ensure that all films are of the same batch. With the big manufacturers, even films for the amateur market are issued within close sensitivity tolerances, but with films of the same type but from different batches, there may be differences of 10 ASA from a nominal 100 ASA. Buying films of the same batch, you avoid the possibility of slight differences in slide density. This advice applies only to slide film, as slight differences in sensitivity are far less important with colour negative or black & white films.

You will find different checking procedures at airports around the world. In some places, baggage for the hold passes through an X-ray track, in others it doesn't. Cabin baggage is either hand or X-ray checked, and the passenger himself usually goes through a metal-detecting arch or is submitted to a hand search. Sometimes hand baggage is given only a metal detection check. X-rays can fog film, and continuous complaints from the travelling public have caused most airport security people

to lower X-ray strength from a previously high and unnecessary level.

For several years now, my own procedure has been to carry all film in a bag, as cabin luggage, and to indicate this to the security checker. It is then invariably checked by hand, and not passed through an X-ray track, where this exists. In certain places, especially in Italian airports, the security people have insisted on my bag of film passing through the X-ray track, insisting that the low level of radiation was unharmful. That is all right if you are passing through just one or two such checks, but the build-up of radiation when checking repeatedly at several airports can produce film fog. That's the theory. In practice, with a great deal of travelling all over the world, from Britain to the Mediterranean, from Japan to Thailand, from Israel to Norway, I've never had a film spoiled yet, and on the average holiday abroad, with baggage checks confined to the one journey each way, there is very little danger, provided you take the precautions I suggest. It is possible to buy film bags made of foil, which are said to protect film from X-rays, though independent checks indicate that the foil just isn't thick enough to deflect a heavy burst of radiation. In case you are in doubt, a metal detector check has no effect on film.

Heat and humidity

Protecting film while on holiday is no problem. If you are away for just a week or so, even in a hot climate, just make sure you don't leave your film in a closed car, especially the glove compartment, which can reach frying temperature. Keep the films as cool as possible, by wrapping them in a garment inside a travel bag, and withdrawing them as required. Only in places like India, and then only during an extended stay of some weeks, is there any danger of bacteria eating into the emulsion of the film. Even in the hottest climate, this danger only exists where there is a high level of humidity.

Most colour films are now bought in small cans with screw or snap-on lids. Don't remove a film from its container until you actually want to load it into the camera, and when fully exposed put the cassette straight back into the container with the lid on tight. Some photographers like to put a small bag of silica gel, the kind packed with cameras and other equipment, among their films. Silica gel is hygroscopic, that is, it absorbs moisture from the air. Thus, if your films were not in individual cans, but packed together in an air sealed, taped box, a bag of silica gel would prevent humidity inside. In a porous bag, on the other hand, the silica gel would actually attract moisture from outside.

For any ordinary holiday of two weeks duration, in a climate *suitable* for a holiday, there's no need to bother about bacteria. Yes, I do know one photographer who fights a constant battle with bacteria. He covers the Far East, and particularly India, for an Asian group of magazines. The bacteria eat not only his films, but his cameras, too, and after every picture story his great worry is getting the films to base, and processed as quickly as possible.

Processing

The longer it is kept, the less sensitive the film becomes. With normal shelf storage of unexposed film, deterioration is slight, and a film exposed when absolutely fresh will not give appreciably different results from one approaching its expiry date, which may be two years after issue. Once the film has been exposed, however, the image begins to lose sensitivity. Many casual photographers leave a film half exposed at the end of one summer, and finish it off the following year. In such a case, the two sets of slides show a definite difference in density.

The holiday traveller need not worry about this, but the best advice is to have the films processed as soon as possible after returning home. A delay of a month will make no appreciable difference.

Novel sights

Have you ever noticed how tourists in your locality snap away madly at things which you consider commonplace? The old town hall, a bus shelter, street signs, a policeman. Unless we train our vision, it is a fact that we pay scant attention to familiar surroundings. When we go abroad, however, we are beset by new and exciting images – and it is the turn of the locals to gape at our enthusiasm for 'the commonplace'. Even the street signs look different. In Greece, the traveller is beguiled by the posters, using ink of a different national standard. In villages, there are coloured blankets and sheets airing from the windows, streets are cobbled, the flowers different. Every country has different sights, shapes and colours, which excite and beguile the holidaymaker.

Naturally, this wealth of new images means that the camera's shutter is clicking incessantly, the number of exposed films mounts up, and the dozen films bought at home, and considered adequate for the whole trip, are used up in a few days. Later, when those hundreds of slides or prints come back from the processor, it's a different matter. "Why on earth did I take that?" The fact is, enthusiasm has outstripped critical vision.

The answer is to study those new sights even more carefully in the viewfinder than one would at home. Ask yourself the question, "Am I taking this just because it is different, or because it has pictorial merit?" Naturally, there are many things you will simply want to record, as happy memories, but when it comes to real pictures, be very selective.

Location portraits

On holiday, you will often want to photograph a companion against an interesting background, perhaps a well-known monument. A common mistake is to pose your companion close to the monument, then retreat with the camera until both monument and companion are included in the viewfinder. Result: one monument, and one tiny speck-sized companion. One sees tourists making this mistake time and again.

The trick is to retreat with the camera to a point where the monument, or whatever, is nicely filling the viewfinder with a satisfying composition, then introduce your companion in the foreground. If you have only a standard lens, keep the figure at about ten feet from the camera. Focus on the figure, stop the lens down well, to f/8 or f/11, and the background detail will be sharp enough. The average compact camera has a slightly wideangle lens, usually around 38mm focal length, and consequently more depth-of-field. With this, the figure can be brought to half-length range, and at the same aperture of f/8 or f/11 the background will still be sharp enough. If you have an SLR with a wideangle lens of, say 35mm or 28mm focal length, the figure can be even closer.

In this way, it is possible to arrange figure and location to form an integrated composition, instead of merely someone standing in front of a background.

Although many people were on the beach, choice of a high viewpoint has isolated the child against an uncluttered background of sand. Kodak Ektachrome film, 6x6cm format.

Under a blue sky reflected from the sea, there may be a blue cast, even if a Skylight filter has been used. For such conditions, the browner Wratten 81A filter, which Japanese manufacturers sometimes call Cloudy, will add warmth to the subject.

10.
Still Life and Flowers

Still life photography is an excellent training ground for technique. With outdoor work slight imperfections in quality are seldom noticed, as they are subservient to the atmosphere and action of the subject. In a still life, technical imperfections appear more obvious, probably because the accent is on fine detail, which causes the viewer to study the photograph more deeply. As far as technique is concerned, any photographer who can achieve quality with a still life, can certainly achieve equal quality outdoors. Even more important, a good still life demands impeccable composition. Working with the subject entirely under his control, the photographer simply has no excuse for faulty composition. He can take as long as he likes to arrange the subject and the lighting. Indoors, clouds, people and animals don't move, and there are no telephone wires and poles to intrude. If a bottle or a lettuce is in the wrong place, it can be shifted an inch or so. If the lettuce looks dry, water can be sprinkled on it. This is why every hour spent studying a subject 'at the table' is worth its weight in outdoor successes.

Subject choice

The material available for still life studies is inexhaustible, and far easier to come by than a good landscape or other outdoor subject. Choice of subject matter gives enormous scope to the imagination, and this in itself is a worthwhile exercise. In the past, still life was often known as table top photography, and tended to be rather twee. Little glass animals, artificial pyramids, lakes made from a mirror surrounded by sand, and so on. There is simply no need to settle for subjects like these. The whole world of plants, fruits and flowers is at one's disposal, providing a never-ending suc-

cession of beautiful subject matter. The still life pictures used in this book are of subjects gleaned from my own garden and larder.

There are also countless man-made objects. Old books with fine bindings, curiously wrought candle-holders and glassware, even kitchen implements. An object doesn't have to be antique, but it should have the integrity of good craftsmanship. There's all the difference in the world between a traditionally-woven corn dolly and a souvenir leprechaun mass-produced for the tourist trade.

The novice often makes the mistake of including unlike objects in a still life, whereas the expert ensures a unity of materials or purpose. For example, there is total unity in a picture constructed of a candle, an old steel-rimmed pair of spectacles, and an ancient volume. If these are standing on a velvet table-cloth, fine; if on a plastic table-top, there is disharmony. Similarly, vegetables or fruit arranged in a wooden trug against old sacking have unity of materials. If the sacking were to be replaced by, say, a girlie calendar, the unity would be broken. That, of course, is an extreme example of what not to do, but I am sure you get the point.

Like goes with like, and no mistakes will be made if you stay with natural subjects, well-crafted objects, and those with similarity of purpose.

A good still life isn't just a matter of putting interesting subject matter on a table and getting a sharp picture of it. A careful distinction has to be made between the aesthetic merit of the subject, and the aesthetic content of the picture made from it. How the photographer forms a setting for the subject, with complementary background, lighting to produce shadows that form part of the composition, and a meaningful use of space – these things determine the

99

For still life subjects it is best to use a slow film and a very small aperture, as every part of the picture will be looked at in detail. Ordinary overhead room lighting here provided a trace of fill-in illumination.

photographer's aesthetic contribution. This is the main reason I prefer to work with organic subjects, and simple, well-crafted objects. To my mind, good pottery forms a better subject than jewellery, and woodware than gold plate.

In outdoor work we aren't always looking for passive composition, and often a feeling of stress may actually strengthen a picture. In still life, this is never the case. The very name implies cohesion and passive harmony. The pictures on pages 100–101 show how the subject matter has been arranged to prevent the viewer's eye wandering out of the margins of the print. As you can see, the easiest way to achieve this is by the circular line. The idea is to arrange items so as to direct the eye towards a central point after touring the detail. It doesn't do to make these guide lines too obvious, as long as the general direction is there.

Lighting

A good thing about still life, as compared to, say, formal portraiture, is that it requires only the simplest lighting. The picture on page 101 was taken on a table close to a window, and no supplementary lights or reflectors were used. Good, strong shadows are essential, on grounds of both contrast and composition, and it is best to work obliquely to the window.

Outdoors, a change in light, as the sun becomes overcast, will have a strong effect on the mood and even the composition (those shadows), but indoors conditions are different. As the light is in any case directional and diffused, this will have little effect other than to cause an increase in exposure. In colour, of course, the picture could look bluish, but this is easily overcome by using a Skylight or Wratten 81A (Cloud) filter.

If the direct rays of the sun strike the subject there will be high contrast and sharp-edged shadows. This is permissible if the photographer feels that this is aiding his composition, but I prefer a somewhat softer shadow with some detail, so prefer to arrange my subjects just beyond the sun's direct rays, or with the light diffused by net curtains, or when a cloud is passing over the sun. As I work in a small room with light walls, there is always sufficient fill-in to avoid empty shadows. If conditions are such that a reflector is needed, try a sheet of white card, or even a white towel draped over a nearby chair. Care must be taken not to take the reflector too close to the shadow side of the subject, otherwise the shadows will lighten too much, and the strength of the composition will be lost. Only the veriest trace of fill-in is needed.

Flash, whether direct, bounced or brolly, is not recommended for still life work, unless it can be linked to a continuous light source in such a way that the effect can be studied and precisely duplicated by the flash. An effective method is to rig up a sheet of semi-transparent polythene, muslin or tracing paper, about 4–5ft from the subject. Use this as a diffuser for a studio lamp placed at least 18in beyond it. When the lighting effect has been arranged satisfactorily, replace the lamp with the flash unit and make the exposure. You will not be able to work in the computer mode, but it is quite easy to estimate the exposure increase required when using the diffuser. Simply take meter readings of the subject with and without the diffuser in place, and apply the difference when using the flash.

Technical

Having taken account of the aesthetic considerations, a good still life also calls for good technique. In the first place, careful attention has to be paid to depth-of-field, as nothing looks worse in a still life than slightly out-of-focus detail. Every part of a still-life picture will be studied by the viewer, and should therefore be sharp. The only permissible exception might be a slight lack of sharpness on the background.

The depth-of-field problem is always acute in close-up work, but it can be overcome by pointing the camera downwards a little, thus lessening the distance to be covered between foreground and background. Even so, f/16 should be considered a standard aperture, and even smaller if your lens will stop down that far.

Most of my own still-life work is done on a Mamiya 645 with the standard lens, and I develop Plus-X in D.76.

This still life was lit by a window on the right. No reflector was used. The strength lies in good texture, contrast, and the series of oval shapes, offset by the angular spoon.

which facilitates the finalising of composition at the enlarging stage. Nevertheless, by working carefully with a 35mm camera, using a really steady tripod, and with accurate development of slow, fine-grained film, equally good results can be obtained.

A D-I-Y still-life table

Every professional studio has its product table, on which still-life shots of everything from jewellery to cosmetics are made. Such tables are usually of thin steel tubing with adjustable joints, and are designed to support various backgrounds. The flat surface is a frame support on which sheets of clear glass or formica can be supported. Such a table permits a whole variety of professional effects which the amateur doesn't know how to simulate, or finds difficulty in setting up. A do-it-yourself version of a product table in wood or Meccano is quite easy to construct.

The standard lighting by which the professional glamorises a product is simpler than you might expect. Often, it consists only of an overhead light, shining directly down on the subject. The extra bit of know-how is to have available black, white, and coloured sheets of formica or melamine. Try standing your subject on one of these, with the one overhead lamp – instant glamour.! With a fine reflection in the formica. You can also use a half-roll of coloured paper to provide a seamless background and base. Don't fall into the trap of expecting black paper to come out dead black, unless it can be set well back out of the light. Closer to the subject it picks up light, and usually has dark grey reflections. The professional uses black velvet, which has better absorption properties.

Flowers indoors

Everything that has been said so far about still life photography also applies to flowers, though more than one light source is often necessary to bring out the translucent texture of many petals and leaves. In nature, it is often difficult to outline the bloom or blooms against a plain background. Too often, there is a profusion of stalks and vegetation to provide an irritating background that causes confusion. Ways of coping with this will be explained in the next section.

Indoors, it is quite easy to isolate the flowers against a plain background. The

To take flower studies as sharp as these, you need a small lens aperture and a tripod. You also have to wait until the flower is perfectly still. Both shots were taken this way, on Kodak Ektachrome film.

diluted 1:1 with water, for the time recommended by Kodak. Full processing details and suggestions are given in Chapter Seventeen. One advantage of working with a format larger than 35mm, is that the image is more easily studied on the focusing screen. Another is that the larger contact print is easier to study and mark up with a Chinagraph pencil, pale blue background paper available for photographic purposes simulates a sky, but any colour or shade can be chosen to give adequate subject contrast.

Perhaps the most difficult shot for the amateur is an arrangement of blooms in a vase. However beautifully they are arranged, there is a world of difference between studying the subject direct, and in a photograph. When looking at the arrangement, we can go closer, go round, appreciate each bloom and curve of stalk and leaf. In the photograph, the entire vase and its contents are included, so each bloom is necessarily small in the picture area. It calls for excellent lighting, a background that will give adequate contrast to the different colours and tones of the subject, and utmost sharpness.

Often, a more satisfying result is obtained by getting closer and limiting the picture to just one or two blooms, which are far more easily composed.

The upper picture was taken with the camera's standard lens set at its closest focusing distance, the lower one using a Hoya close-up supplementary lens of +1 dioptre.

There is no reason why just the lip of the vase should not be included instead of the whole.

Flowers outdoors

On a bright day it is usually possible to take excellent flower studies outdoors, without the help of a tripod. Working very close, the lens has to be well stopped down in order to obtain sharp coverage of near and far petals, and this is not possible with hand-held exposures unless the light and the film speed permit a fast enough shutter speed.

Naturally, a great many amateurs also love flowers, and are content to record the blooms that appeal to them without worrying overmuch about confusing backgrounds, pictorial lighting, and so on. Many photographers, for example, are content to work with a small flashgun and a medium telephoto lens. The speed of the flash and the very small apertures required, ensure pictures which are pin-sharp from front to rear. Naturally, the lighting is flat and does little to reveal delicate texture, but in most cases the results are satisfactory.

The amateur concerned to get the professional results one sees in photo and gardening magazines, however, needs to take a bit more trouble.

Often, the advanced worker or the professional uses a windbreak which can be very easily constructed from four lengths of wood dowel sharpened at one end, and a length of strong material. In use, this acts as both windbreak and background. Even on the stillest day, flowers tend to wave gently on their stalks, which becomes instantly obvious when studying the viewfinder or screen. Photographed at a distance, this slight movement is negligible, but in close-up it calls for a fairly fast exposure. The windbreak allows the bloom to come to rest and makes the photographer's work much easier. With a wind blowing, the windbreak becomes an essential part of the flower photographer's equipment and certainly no trouble to carry with him.

The material used for the windbreak can be varied. I have seen them made from almost opaque cloth, light grey on one side, dark on the other, to suit different blooms. The kind I think most useful are made from strong translucent polythene, which diffuses the natural background but does not alter its colour. For a particular effect, a sheet of coloured paper or cloth can be draped over the back section of the windbreak.

With a windbreak in position and isolating the bloom or blooms from a confused background, it is relatively easy to make hand-held exposures, though the professional, with his bigger camera, will invariably use a tripod. Of course, not every photographer wants his picture to be sharp from front to rear. Artistically, it may be preferable to have out-of-focus petals and leaves curving towards the camera, providing just blobs of colour. The photographer may even decide that he wants just the stamens sharp, surrounded by an out-of-focus swirl of colour. Whatever kind of picture is required, it should be borne in mind that the area of sharpness should be purposely controlled, not left to the vagaries of wind and camera shake.

11.
Children and Animals

Children and animals are two of the most rewarding subjects for the amateur. Sitting still, they present no problems, but when they get into action, which seems to be most of the time, they call for a lively response and a high level of preparedness on the part of the photographer. With either, it is best to start out with a clear idea of the kind of results you are after. A portrait in repose calls for one technique; an action shot of the subject haring round the garden calls for another.

Children

Success in child photography depends on one commodity you cannot buy in a photo store, and that is a liking for your subjects. If the child is your own, of course, you are bound to like it, but only a saint could honestly answer that he or she likes *all* children. After all, children have variously been described as little innocents, little monsters, and ungrown adults. One thing you can be quite sure of, and that is that any child instantly recognises the true feelings of a photographer. If you don't really like children, or feel uneasy in their company, your most convincing smile will be met with a blank, if not hostile, stare. If you like them, or at least feel easy in their presence, they will soon accept you.

Children differ enormously, from age to age, and from family to family, but there are some general tips which the prospective child photographer would do well to heed.

Babies

Having photographed some thousands of children, both professionally and as an ordinary amateur masochist, my definition of a baby is simple but practical: a baby is a small animated object not yet having reached the crawling stage. Its parents consider it the most beautiful thing in the world. Every windy grimace is interpreted as a smile, and it has an uncanny knack of blinking, turning its head away, or drooling, just at the moment you press the shutter release. Seriously, I like babies.

Until a baby is three months old, posing is limited to tummy-on-the-rug shots, and these are best taken without even a nappy. The line of the little back and bottom are best shown this way. A call from Mum will usually make baby lift his head for a moment, and that's the moment to catch. If the baby cannot yet lift its head, it will rest it sideways on rug or blanket, which is also good for photography. Lying-on-the-back shots are seldom as pleasing.

Most babies can sit up, and take notice, at six months, and this is probably the best age. Features are better formed, and expressions more prolific. If baby is still a bit tottery, and liable to topple over, there's an old professional trick that always scores. Mum supports baby with her hands hidden by a fold of blanket, but keeps her body out of the picture.

Toddlers

Once the child has started to crawl and toddle, you need a more flexible technique. Flash or strong lighting is required, not only to allow fast shutter speeds to be used, but to make rapid focusing easier.

It is always best to allow some time for the child to get used to your presence, and turn its attention away from your equipment. Keep your lighting stands, if you use them, close to the wall, and preferably protected from little hands by a heavy armchair or table. The advantage of working indoors is that the child's movements are limited. You soon will

Keep 'em still! The trick in candids of children is to ensure that the right expression and the focus coincide. Do this by pre-focusing on the right spot, and providing something to keep the child still for a moment. The baby with the frilly pants stopped long enough to examine an object held by the older girl and the photographer was ready. Young Sarah leaned forward to sniff the flower, which was already in focus. A child held in its mother's arms is easy to focus on. Blowing a dandelion clock gave Rachel something to do— long enough for the shot to be composed and taken.

discover the regular tracks and favoured places, and this will facilitate fast focusing. The oldest trick in the book is to place a favourite toy on the carpet, and get Mum to put the child in position. The toy will hold its attention for a few seconds at least, so be ready to shoot. Once a child has lost interest in an object, no amount of coaxing will help. And re-member, small children stay interested in nothing for very long.

Shooting by daylight in the garden avoids lighting problems, but you'll still need a certain amount of ingenuity to ensure that you are focused on the right spot at the right time. One trick is to pre-focus on a certain point, then get Mum to call the child from such a position that the child will cross that point. Many modern SLRs have an autowind attachment, taking two frames per second. Thus, if it takes the toddler, say, four seconds to reach Mum's outstretched arms, you can get a sequence of eight action shots. There is no better way to depict those endearing arm and leg movements, short of using a movie camera. A set of eight small prints mounted in a strip will bring joy to any parents—and the editors of many women's and photo magazines, too.

Whether shooting indoors or out, watch the background and keep it as simple as possible. Above all, and especially with very small children, remember that the best time to photograph is soon after waking and feeding, when the child will be wide awake and happy for an hour or so. Once tiredness or hunger have set in, pack up and come back another day.

Where babies are concerned, don't just content yourself with the whole child.

Come in close for a few head shots, and take some smaller details of little hands and feet. These are details that fascinate parents, and will certainly build your reputation as a baby photographer with a good eye.

Helpers

If the whole family want to crowd in on a shooting session, be quite firm. One helper only, and this will usually be Mum. If two or more people are present, in the excitement of the moment the baby will be trying to make up its mind which way to look. With cootchee-coo coming from one direction, and chick-a-chick-a-chick from another, baby risks a split personality, and so do your pictures.

You may want Mum, off camera to the left, to call and wave a favourite toy, hoping for a quick smile. If Dad calls from another direction at the same time (and he will), you've no chance. To get a good angle on a small child, you will often have to go down on your knees, or even your stomach, and so will your helper. If the helper calls the child from a much higher position, all you will get is good pictures of the underside of chin and nostrils.

It is amazing how small children take to cameras, and want to adopt them as toys. I've endured more than one bawling session because I wouldn't hand over my shiny camera. It is best to spend the first few minutes after the child has been brought into the room or outdoor shooting area, just chatting to Mum, with the camera well in sight of the child, but safely held. Even if the child wants to investigate, it will usually turn its attention to other interesting objects and the work of photography can then start. Even when photographing your own child, it is far better to have a helper than try working alone. You'll be able to get smiles and waves directed to one side, instead of always towards the camera. It is also a fact that even the best behaved toddlers have an uncanny instinct for playing up a parent-photographer, and always at the critical moment. Help is almost essential, but do remember, only one helper.

Money-making children

Many an amateur makes a useful amount of money by photographing the children of friends and acquaintances. If you want to enter this field, it is important to draw a distinction between the kind of child pictures you like to take, and the kind that the parents would like. Often, the two coincide, but sometimes they can be very different. Some Mums like to keep their children beautifully dressed and spotlessly clean, and want them photographed that way. They would shudder at a lively portrait of a grinning, dirt-spattered urchin, or one with ice-cream smeared all over its face. Other Mums are just the opposite and, I am glad to say, appear to be more in the majority these days.

The professional often starts out with shots of the clean, neat child in fairly reposed and conventional situations, after which he goes for the grubby but delightful true-to-life shots. Do the same, and if Mum starts to express doubts return to the more traditional approach. The modern Mum knows that her child and dirt usually have an irresistible attraction for each other, and will seldom take this line. Carry a bar of chocolate with you. A couple of squares of this placed in a toddler's hand always leads to the most natural of all child pictures, complete with dirty face and fingers. What's more, the child's concentration on the chocolate gives you plenty of time to focus and get your sequence. Never, never, give the chocolate to the child yourself. If Mum agrees, hand the chocolate to her, and let her give it to the child. It could happen that a bit might go down the wrong way and cause a choking fit, and you don't want to get ordered from the house as a potential child murderer. Don't laugh at such a fanciful concept. The advice is based on experience!

Animals

Basically, animals can be divided into two categories, zoo and domestic. Properly approached, either sort will provide truly rewarding pictures. Where zoo animals are concerned, there is seldom any need for the photographer to establish good rapport with his subject, but domestic animals can respond in much the same way as children. It isn't always necessary to like a particular domestic animal, as long as the owner is there to control it, thus allowing the photographer to concentrate on his viewfinder.

Photographing animals of either kind, zoo or domestic, can provide an amazing lesson in grace and relaxation, beyond the achievement of even the most adept yoga exponent. Animals, with the possible exception of overfed and under-exercised pets, move gloriously and relax superbly, all by instinct. This, indeed, is amazing grace. A good animal picture, whether taken at a zoo or in the home, always shows one aspect of this quality.

At the zoo

In most urban zoos you are often restricted in your choice of background, and in the angle from which you shoot. Nevertheless, many a good exhibition picture was shot in a zoo, simply by applying a little know-how.

The wire of cages and enclosures is sometimes an obstacle to good pictures. If the mesh is large enough, it is often possible to aim the lens through an opening, and obtain an unobstructed view. If the mesh is too fine for this, you

These two kittens were sitting on a bread bin, when their attention was held by a dangled scrap of silver paper on a string. Twin flash was used.

can make it 'disappear' simply by putting the lens close against it. It is best to have the front element practically touching the mesh, and this will mean removing the lenshood if you are using one. Be careful, however, not to scratch the lens. Usually the front element is sufficiently recessed to avoid this, but care must be taken if the front element is flush with the rim of the mount, or of very convex shape. The risk is totally avoided if you fit a UV or Skylight filter to the lens. Even with the sun shining the slight extra warmth imparted to colour film by the filter will do no harm, and you can be sure that the valuable lens will be safe.

The disappearing effect on the wire mesh is greatest when a telephoto lens is used. With a standard lens, ensure that only a couple of centimetres separates lens and mesh, and don't use too small an aperture, say, not below f/5.6, otherwise the increased depth of field may cause a telltale blurred mesh pattern to overlie the subject. Even this is seldom obtrusive. A wideangle lens is least suitable for the purpose, and should be used at the widest possible aperture.

Big cats

Trying to take pictures in the lion and tiger houses is usually a waste of time. You can't get close enough to aim the camera between the bars, and in any case a champed-up camera would defeat the skills of any repairman. Lighting is usually too dull to permit shots of the poor beasts stalking up and down, and the best you can hope for is the head of a bored animal behind iron bars. The bigger urban zoos have an enclosure for the big cats, separated from the on-lookers by a wide trench, and it is in this

109

situation that you will get your best shots. Naturally, a telephoto lens is essential if you want close-ups, and lenses of 135mm to 300mm focal length will be found most useful. There was a time when a good telephoto cost a great deal of money, but nowadays, thanks to computer technology, 300MS and telephotos are available from independent optical companies at a very reasonable price. Anyone thinking of specialising in zoo photography must consider such a lens an essential part of his equipment.

The enclosures usually provide a very good setting, if not an entirely natural one, for the animals they contain. Often they are backed by a wall of stone, and there is always at least one position where railings, people and other unwanted detail can be excluded. Not only the big cats, but bears, pandas and the bigger monkeys can be found in such trenched enclosures.

Small enclosures

The bigger, but less fierce, animals, such as zebra, bison and wildebeest, as well as emus, ostriches and secretary birds, usually have a small enclosure fenced off in front of their houses. These fences are usually only waist high, and present no obstacle to your camera.

True, the animal's house in the background precludes any attempt at a perfectly natural setting, but with a really good picture of the animal this is often acceptable. One good trick is to use a telephoto at a very wide aperture, which will put the background well out of focus.

The aquarium

Fish tanks are always lit from above, and the light filtering down through the water diffuses to give an excellent lighting effect. The trouble is, aquarium lighting is fairly dim, which is the way the fish like it, and even with 3M's 640T film exposures are likely to be in the region of 1/15sec or 1/30sec at f/2.8. This is all right if you have an SLR, perhaps with close-up lens fitted, pressed against the glass, and provided you've chosen one of those fish that obligingly stop and pose for a few seconds. You can even use flash, and if the lens is pressed against the glass there will be no danger of flashback. However, not all zoos permit the use of flash, though exceptions are sometimes made in particular areas, so

do ask the keeper first. An ill-directed flash will frighten, and possibly cause injury to, a subject that is not used to bright light.

If you are using colour for your trip to the zoo, you will almost certainly have chosen daylight type film. In the aquarium, with the tanks lit by artificial light, and the water often green, your results could have an unpleasant orange or green colour. Using a blue 80B conversion filter will get rid of the orange, but you may still be surprised to find your slides coming back with a green cast. The effect is probably an accurate rendition of the colours present in the tank, but only in the clearest water can you expect the fish to show up well against a neutral background. The specialist, of course, is able to rig up flash directly above the tank, and will only take pictures just after the inside of the glass has had its weekly scrub clean of algae.

Zoo parks

Undoubtedly, the best hunting ground for the animal photographer is an African game reserve, and if you can afford the money such a trip provides opportunities for unforgettable studies. Not far behind, are the big zoo or nature parks, within reach of nearly all major cities. Here, the animals have vastly more freedom of movement than in urban zoos, and usually there has been an attempt to provide settings closely resembling the animals' natural habitats. As such parks are in the country, the shots you take are seldom spoiled by distant buildings or telegraph poles, and there are many opportunities for taking outstanding studies of the various denizens.

There is often a dolphinarium, with secondary entertainment provided by that most beautiful of all beasts, the killer whale. If you attend one of these sessions, get in early and occupy a front seat at the side, not in front. Then, as the dolphins or whale leap from the water to take food or perform their aerobatics, you can get them against a clear sky or trees, without the keeper or feeder being in the picture.

Simply because there is such a wealth of subjects at a zoo, the novice is sometimes tempted to shoot away wildly, without the care he would take with a single landscape view. The result can be a disappointing series of snapshots without much pictorial merit. To get really good pictures, walk round the zoo

Kitten among the cabbages. A nice subject, but the cabbage leaves are confusing. A black line was added to contain the picture.

first, noting the backgrounds, angles, and the position of the sun. A certain setting may look very drab in the morning, but by the afternoon the sun will have moved, casting the background into shadow and backlighting the animal in a particular enclosure.

It is far better to photograph only a few animals at each visit. This will give you time to study the subject, and anticipate and prepare for the moment when the animal will be in the best position for a shot, and with a suitably contrasting background.

Domestic animals

People love pets, but I often think the word is a bit of a put-down for animals which have as much personality as their owners, and often far more grace and energy. Cats are quite easy to photograph, though the beginner often contents himself with a shot of puss curled up in an armchair with a distracting pattern. Slightly more adventurous is the close-up of the cat's face, with every whisker and the dilated pupils pin-sharp under the searching speed of a flash. As the cat's face is fairly flat and what matters is the pattern of fur, flash-on-camera is adequate for this kind of shooting. If you use

a telephoto lens for your close-ups, the flash will be far enough away not to require an aperture smaller than your lens will stop down to.

Tabbies, Siamese and other mid-toned cats are the easiest to photograph, as they stand out well against almost any background. White cats are best photo-graphed against a mid-toned back-ground, as black offers the strongest contrast and the effect looks rather com-mercial. Of course, a white cat can be effectively photographed against a white background, and the pink eyes of the albino look quite brilliant when sur-rounded by white in a colour picture. Remember that your exposure meter will try to reduce white to mid-grey, so give at least half a stop more exposure than the meter indication.

Cats outdoors

The usual image of the pet cat is that of a lazy or comfort-loving creature curled up on a lap or in front of a fire. In fact, cats have an instinct for healthy exercise, and present far more variety of form when photographed outdoors. Apart from the occasional lucky shot when a cat is grooming itself on a wall and you have a camera handy, it is useful to study the daily routine of your pet. Watch for those parts of the garden or street where puss habitually stops for a sniff round, or explores the pecking perimeter of next door's pet. Try to anticipate her arrival at these points, get in position, and pre-focus.

With the aid of a helper, it is quite easy to take those apparently difficult shots of the cat filling the frame and walking towards the camera. Simply lie flat, pre-focus on the right spot, get your helper to stand behind you and call the cat. An offer of a bit of food may be necessary.

If your cat has an amenable disposition and will sit still while you photograph her, you can add extra interest by getting her to lick her lips. Simply get your helper to dab the merest trace of fish-paste beside puss's mouth, and she'll lick away to your heart's content. Working with cats in Britain, many's the time I've blessed Mother Shippam's paste. Perhaps this is known variously in France, Germany and the United States as Mère Shippams, Mutter Shippams, and Grannie Shippams. At all events, it does wonders for cat control!

Pups

The photography of dogs and puppies is essentially the same as that of cats and kittens, but there is one important difference. Whereas the feline moves carefully and (except under stress) avoids knocking things over, the average canine in a studio is like the proverbial bull in a china shop.

Part of the charm of puppies is their floppy clumsiness, which is fine for pictures, but just make sure you don't leave your equipment lying about. A pup thinks nothing of chewing through a flash lead or lighting cable – not until his teeth reach bare wire, that is. They have a friendly habit of rushing up and giving the camera lens an affectionate lick, and an equally devastating habit of either worrying or christening things. When a pup has had enough play he will flop down, and shortly indulge in an almighty yawn. Be ready for it.

The easiest dogs to photograph are the really dignified ones, such as wolf-hounds, Great Danes, airedales, and the like. It is beneath their contempt to dash around aimlessly, and they often pose in royal manner. Don't get too close to a dog if he is standing three-quarters on to the camera, if you have only a standard lens. The perspective effect will be exaggerated, with large head and small hindquarters. The best effect is obtained by going back a few feet and using a telephoto lens. On the other hand, a dog photographed broadside on with a standard lens, will look perfectly natural.

Although most dog owners want fun pictures of their pets, the owner of a show dog will want you to reveal the finer points of the animal, such as the prick of the ears, the set of head on neck, width of shoulder and chest, stance of the legs, and so on. Unless you are an expert fancier, rely on the owner to position the dog for you.

12.
Taking Close-ups

Most SLR cameras have a standard lens that will focus as close as eighteen inches. Other types of camera usually have a closest focusing distance of about three feet. This is adequate for a great deal of out-and-about photography, but there are many occasions when you want to get closer. With an SLR there are four ways to achieve this. First, by using a special macro lens, capable of reproducing the subject half-size on the film. Second, by using a supplementary close-up lens that screws in front of the camera lens. Third, by means of extension tubes which fit between the lens and camera. Fourth, by means of an extension bellows, which also fits between lens and camera. The only one of these aids that can be successfully used with a non-SLR

A simple close-up lens is the quickest and easiest way to get close to a small subject. These supplementary lenses can be had in various strengths.

A set of extension tubes, used singly or in combination between SLR camera and lens, permits close focusing down to a ratio of about 1:1 (same size), and is more versatile than a set of supplementary close-up lenses.

With a 50 ASA film and a telephoto fitted with an extension tube, 1/30sec at f/5.6 was risky business. The shot is only just sharp enough for reproduction.

compact camera is the supplementary lens.

An optical device, known as an Auto-Up (Japanese) is available for certain compact cameras. This consists of a supplementary close-up lens and a parallax-compensating wedge held in a frame. When fitted to the camera, the supplementary lens covers the camera lens and the wedge in turn covers the viewfinder, thus enabling the rangefinder to continue operating over a range from three feet down to about eighteen inches, or less, according to the strength of the supplementary lens.

The most modestly-priced, and easiest to use, of all close-focusing aids, is the supplementary lens, and later in this chapter I will describe a simple means by which correct focus can be obtained when using one in conjunction with a compact camera.

Getting closer

Supplementary lenses are available in several strengths, and a set of extension tubes, or rings, includes tubes of varying

To reveal the subtle glaze in this bowl by English potter Roy Evans, the photograph was taken outdoors in the direct rays of the sun. A close-up supplementary lens was used over the camera's standard lens.

Jewelry usually shows up best against a dark background, and needs careful lighting. Exposure is best obtained by using a grey card or incident light meter (see Chapter Five), and then bridging one stop either way for safety. Kodachrome film.

lengths. The pictures on pages 116–117 show the different degrees of magnification that can be obtained with the more popular supplementary lenses. There are usually four extension tubes making up a set, and these can be used singly or in combination. With all four tubes together, same-size, or 1:1 magnification can be obtained directly on the film.

There are two important differences between supplementary lenses and extension tubes. First, supplementary lenses do not affect the exposure. Extension tubes do. The greater the tube length, the bigger the increase in exposure necessary to compensate for the dimmer image received by the film. At 1:1 magnification, for example, four times extra exposure (2 stops larger, or 2 shutter speed values slower) is required.

Second, when using extension tubes, it is possible to vary the camera-subject distance over a wide range. This distance is limited when using a supplementary lens.

It has often been suggested that extension tubes are preferable to supplementary lenses, as the former do not affect the optical qualities of the camera lens. This is not true in practice. The camera lens, unless it is a special macro design, is computed to give its best performance at middle and far distances. Used close-up, the residual aberrations of the lens are increased and sharpness is not so good. This does not mean to say that the quality that can be obtained with

a camera lens on extension tubes is not satisfactory. The supplementary lens works in a different way, by altering the focal length of the lens to which it is attached. If the camera lens is stopped down to, say, f/11, the image obtained with a supplementary will without doubt be just as good as that obtained with extension tubes.

In its favour, the supplementary lens is quicker in use, does not interfere with automatic linkages between lens and camera, is more compact than a tube, and all those which are now supplied by well-known makers are of good optical quality.

Perspective

When you fit an extension tube between camera body and lens, you are simply extending the forward focusing movement of the lens, which allows you to move closer to the subject. The greater the extension, the closer you can get. It follows that the closer you approach the subject, the more exaggerated the perspective will appear in the picture.

With a supplementary lens, magnification of the image is due to the strength of the supplementary, not to the camera-to-subject distance. In fact, this distance will remain fixed for any particular supplementary, when the camera lens is set at Infinity. For magnifications above, say, 1:4, perspective is often more pleasing, because less pronounced, when using a supplementary.

latter conveys to the lens the auto-diaphragm and metering facilities of the camera, while with the former it is necessary to stop the lens down manually, and often to determine the exposure independently of the SLRs TTL-metering system.

When working within two or three inches of the subject accurate focusing is sometimes possible only by moving the complete camera-bellows-lens set-up towards or away from the subject. To facilitate this movement, the best bellows units run on a sliding stage. The necessary movement may be a mere millimetre or so, and to achieve this without a sliding stage is very difficult. It is, for example, almost impossible to make the minute adjustment by shifting the legs of a tripod. Cheap bellows units are not to be recommended, as even the screw-lock can sometimes shift the lens out of focus.

The best bellows units incorporate scales for one or more lenses, indicating the exposure increase factor that must be applied for any degree of magnification. This is useful even when working with an automatic camera, as the dimness of the image at extreme magnification

Bellows unit

A bellows unit consists of bellows running on a track. At the front is a standard to which the camera lens is attached, while a rear standard fits the throat of the SLR camera body. It works in the same way as a set of extension tubes, except that magnification is continuous and covers a far greater range. Like extension tubes, bellows can be manual or automatic. The

A bellows unit between camera and lens gives greater extension than a set of tubes, and magnification is continuous and variable. The stage underneath enables the entire camera-bellows to be moved slightly in relation to the subject.

The top picture opposite was taken with the lens of a compact 35mm camera set at its closest focusing distance of 3ft. The following pairs show the effect with close-up supplementary lenses of +2, +3 and +4 dioptres (*left*) with the lens set at Infinity, and (*right*) set to the closest focusing distance.

may be beyond the sensitivity of the metering system. If you are forced to take the meter reading at full aperture, you will still need to know how much extra exposure to give.

The instructions packed with each set of extension tubes give similar information for any one tube or combination.

Technique

The camera must be rock steady when taking close-ups, as the slightest movement will mean lack of sharpness. This is no problem when working outdoors in good light with a supplementary lens or short extension tube, and a fairly fast

With an SLR the lens can be focused on the viewfinder screen, but there is no screen on a compact SLR. By photographing an inclined sheet of newspaper this girl has determined the points of true focus with supplementary lenses in use. She has then measured the distances from the camera back and tied knots at these distances in a length of string. With any supplementary lens, she can now obtain the right distance, drop the string, and take a sharp picture.

shutter speed. However, if the camera is hand-held, it must be remembered that you need to sway only a few millimetres backwards or forwards after focusing, and sharpness will be lost. The best technique is to focus the lens first, take a half pressure on the shutter release button, then finalise focus by moving the camera slightly, forward or backwards. The exposure can be made at the instant the image appears quite sharp in the viewfinder.

When using non-automatic extension tubes, the lens has to be stopped down manually before making the exposure. In all but the brightest light, this makes it difficult to discern the sharpest point of focus, and for this reason alone automatic tubes are recommended wherever possible. Failing that, a tripod will make the job much easier.

When taking close-ups indoors, and especially at higher magnifications when a bellows unit is used, it is imperative that the camera should vibrate as little as possible during the exposure. Vibration can be caused by any or all of five factors: (1) the action of the mirror-lift of the SLR, (2) shutter jerk, (3) a flimsy tripod, (4) vibration through the floor, and (5) pressure of the finger on the release button, or imparted by too short a cable release.

The first cause can be eliminated in some cameras, where the mirror can be lifted before the exposure. The second can be reduced. If you are using studio lamps, first set up the lighting, focus and compose, determine the exposure and set aperture and shutter speed. Switch off both studio and room lights. Open the camera on Time, or on B by means of a locking cable release. Wait until all vibration has ceased, just a second or so, then make the exposure by switching the studio lamps on and off. Finally, close the shutter.

A flimsy tripod is often worse than no tripod. It can be steadied by hanging a weight underneath, and many a household iron has been pressed into service (if you'll pardon the pun) for this purpose. A good rule is that a tripod for a 35mm or 6 × 6cm camera should weigh about 5lb. Although most tripods now have rubber pads for indoor use, as well as spikes for outdoor work, it is best to use the spikes when working on a carpet. There will be less movement. It takes an SLR about half a second to 'settle down' after the shutter has been opened; that is, for vibration to cease. We can make use of this fact by giving longer, rather than shorter, exposures. The camera may be vibrating during half an exposure of 1sec, but if the exposure is increased to, say, 5sec, the amount of vibration will be negligible.

When using a short cable release for a time exposure, you may find the cable actually pushing or pulling the camera.

For this reason, a cable release should not be shorter than nine inches, and should be curved when used.

Flash, which is fully covered in the next chapter, ensures sharp close-ups. With two or more flashguns you can duplicate the lighting obtained with studio lamps, but even with a single flash and a reflector satisfying results can be achieved. Naturally, any exposure increase factor occasioned by lens extension has to be compensated for, and the various methods are also described in the next chapter.

Close-ups with compacts

The main thing to remember about a supplementary lens, sold in photo stores as close-up lenses, is that when fitted to a camera lens set at Infinity, focus will be sharp at a distance equal to the focal length of the supplementary lens alone. This holds good whatever the focal length of the camera lens. Thus, if you know the focal length of the supplementary, that is the distance you have to measure between the subject and the film plane of the camera.

A stumbling block is that supplementaries are usually marked with the power in diopters ($+1$, $+2$, $+3$, $+4$, and so on),

Using a split-field lens, which is half a close-up lens in a mount, you can get both background and near foreground sharp. You must arrange the picture so that the tell-tale soft centre line is not over a detailed area. Here, it is on the man's left cheek.

These tables show the subject size, film-to-subject distance, magnification, and exposure increase factor, for lenses of various focal lengths, used in conjunction with one or more extension tubes. Such information is often but not always, provided with the set of tubes you buy.

28mm (Distance scale set at 0.4m)

Extension tube combination	Subject size		Film-to-subject distance		Magnification	Exposure factor
	cm	*inches*	*cm*	*inches*		
Not used	39.9 × 26.6	15.72 × 10.48	40.11	15.80	0.09	× 1.1
1	8.5 × 5.7	3.35 × 2.25	16.19	6.38	0.42	× 1.6
2	4.8 × 3.2	1.89 × 1.26	14.17	5.58	0.76	× 2.3
3	3.3 × 2.2	1.30 × 0.87	13.97	5.50	1.09	× 3.0
1+3	2.5 × 1.7	0.99 × 0.67	14.31	5.64	1.42	× 3.8
2+3	2.0 × 1.4	0.79 × 0.55	14.88	5.86	1.76	× 4.7
1+2+3	1.7 × 1.1	0.67 × 0.43	15.57	6.13	2.09	× 5.7

35mm (Distance scale set at 0.45m)

Extension tube combination	Subject size		Film-to-subject distance		Magnification	Exposure factor
	cm	*inches*	*cm*	*inches*		
Not used	37.8 × 25.2	14.9 × 9.9	45.0	17.7	0.10	× 1.2
1	9.8 × 6.5	3.9 × 2.6	18.7	7.4	0.37	× 1.6
2	5.6 × 3.8	2.2 × 1.5	15.6	6.2	0.64	× 2.2
3	4.0 × 2.6	1.58 × 1.02	14.9	5.89	0.91	× 2.9
1+3	3.0 × 2.0	0.18 × 0.79	14.98	5.90	1.18	× 3.6
2+3	2.5 × 1.7	0.99 × 0.67	15.38	6.06	1.45	× 4.4
1+2+3	2.1 × 1.4	0.83 × 0.55	15.95	6.28	1.72	× 5.3

5 mm (Distance scale set at 0.45m)

Extension tube combination	Subject size		Film-to-subject distance		Magnification	Exposure factor
	cm	*inches*	*cm*	*inches*		
Not used	25.0 × 16.7	9.85 × 6.58	45.02	17.74	0.14	× 1.2
1	10.8 × 7.2	4.26 × 2.84	26.15	10.30	0.33	× 1.6
2	6.9 × 4.6	2.72 × 1.81	21.63	8.52	0.52	× 1.9
3	5.1 × 3.4	2.01 × 1.34	20.02	7.89	0.71	× 2.3
1+3	4.0 × 2.7	1.49 × 1.06	19.48	7.68	0.90	× 2.8
2+3	3.3 × 2.2	1.30 × 0.87	19.46	7.67	1.09	× 3.3
1+2+3	2.8 × 1.9	1.10 × 0.75	19.72	7.77	1.28	× 3.8

1 5mm (Distance scale set at 1.2m)

Extension tube combination	Subject size		Film-to-subject distance		Magnification	Exposure factor
	cm	*inches*	*cm*	*inches*		
Not used	33.2 × 22.1	13.08 × 8.71	120.05	47.30	0.11	× 1.3
1	18.1 × 12.1	7.13 × 4.77	76.92	30.31	0.20	× 1.7
2	12.4 × 8.3	4.89 × 3.27	61.36	24.18	0.29	× 2.0
3	9.5 × 6.3	3.74 × 2.48	53.66	21.14	0.38	× 2.4
1+3	7.7 × 5.1	3.03 × 2.01	49.29	19.42	0.47	× 2.8
2+3	6.4 × 4.3	2.52 × 1.69	46.64	18.38	0.56	× 3.3
1+2+3	5.5 × 3.7	2.17 × 1.46	44.99	17.72	0.65	× 3.8

135mm (Distance scale set at 1.5m)

Extension tube combination	Subject size		Film-to-subject distance		Magnification	Exposure factor
	cm	*inches*	*cm*	*inches*		
Not used	45.5 × 30.4	17.93 × 11.8	200.01	78.80	0.08	× 1.3
1	24.1 × 16.1	9.49 × 6.34	120.51	47.48	0.15	× 1.6
2	16.4 × 10.9	6.46 × 4.29	92.53	36.46	0.22	× 1.9
3	12.4 × 8.3	4.89 × 3.27	78.58	30.96	0.29	× 2.2
1+3	10.0 × 6.7	3.94 × 2.64	70.45	27.76	0.36	× 2.5
2+3	8.4 × 5.6	3.31 × 2.21	65.28	25.72	0.43	× 2.9
1+2+3	7.2 × 4.8	2.84 × 1.89	61.83	24.36	0.50	× 3.3

rather than with the actual focal length. The answer is simple. Just divide 100 by the diopters and you have the focal length in cms. Thus:

$$+1 = 100cm$$
$$+2 = 50cm$$
$$+3 = 33.3cm$$
$$+4 = 25cm$$

So, provided you measure that distance correctly, and ensure that the camera lens is set to Infinity, your compact camera is equipped for close-up photography. All you need is a length of nylon string (ordinary string is too stretchy) with a knot tied at the right subject-to-film plane distance. More than one close-up lens, more than one knot.

Just about every compact camera focuses down to 3ft, or 1m, which is 100cm, so there is not much point in using a $+1$ supplementary on a compact. True, if you focus the camera lens closer than Infinity you can move the camera closer to magnify the image. However, the increase in magnification is no more than you can get with a $+2$ and the camera lens at Infinity.

With an SLR, of course, there is no reason why you shouldn't use a supplementary with the camera lens at any distance setting, as you can observe a continuous range of focus. With the compact, you can't do this. It would mean having a knot in the string to tally with every camera lens setting, which is complicated and misleading.

It is far better to use just two settings, (a) with the camera lens at Infinity, and (b) at its closest focusing distance. At the Infinity setting, there is no need for experiment. Just tie the knot at the focal length of the supplementary. If you do want to extend the range, you will have to discover the subject-to-film plane distance with the camera lens set at its closest focusing distance. There are two

ways of doing this. The simplest is to set up a sheet of newspaper on a card, at an inclined angle, and receding from the camera. Expose a frame, develop it, and note the point where the type is sharpest. Run your length of string from the camera back straight to this point, and tie your knot.

A more accurate method is to use a groundglass focusing screen. You set up the camera on a tripod, back open, in front of a movable subject. A bright book cover stood upright on a table is as good a subject as any. The focusing screen is placed in contact with the guide rails, and the book moved back and forth while you examine the screen image with a magnifier. Of course, you'll have to cover the camera and your head with a jacket or cloth, or work in a room with just the book illuminated.

First question: where do you obtain a 35mm focusing screen? The bigger photo stores may have one in stock, or will order one. In the UK they are available at small cost from Polysales Photographic Limited, Polysales House, The Wharf, Godalming, Surrey GU7 1JX.

Provided you take care, you can make a focusing screen from stiff greaseproof or tracing paper. Remember that the screen has to lie in the same plane as the film, which rests *on* the guide rails, not between them. So, cut the paper to the width of the guide rails and fit it in place with a tiny smear of Cow gum or latex cement, which can easily be rubbed off afterwards. It is essential that the paper is taut and dead flat.

Measuring

When tying the knot or knots in your string, make sure that tying the knot has not added a centimetre or so to the length, as focusing has to be quite critical in

When doing close-ups with an SLR camera and macro lens or extension tubes (but not with supplementary close-up lenses) place this chart in the subject plane with the left-hand side aligned with the left-hand short side of the screen. Where the right-hand edge of the screen cuts the chart you can read off the exposure increase factor. Naturally, a TTL-metering camera will allow for the exposure increase, if the light is bright enough for the meter to work.

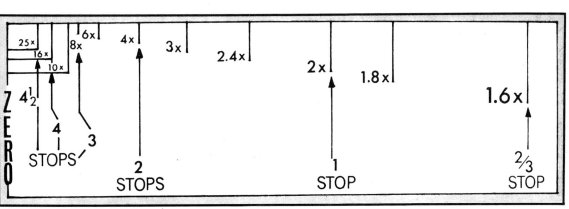

close-up work, even with the slightly wideangle lens of the compact. I have tried two different makes of supplementary lenses, of $+2$ to $+4$ diopter, and have achieved accurate focus at the Infinity setting, without going through the procedure just described – simply by tying knots at the focal length of each supplementary. In the field, proceed as indicated by the pictures on page 118. Holding the cord level with the camera back, stretch out to the subject, drop the knotted end, keep the camera still, and shoot.

Parallax

The viewfinder of a compact camera indicates the same field as is included by the lens, but from a slightly different angle. The difference is unimportant for general work, but with the camera focused at 3ft, you are in danger of cutting off the top of a head. In order to counteract this a pair of parallax marks are normally included in the viewfinder, thus obliging you to move the camera slightly sideways or up or down, depending on whether you are taking horizontal or vertical shots.

When using a supplementary you will be well below 3ft, and all you need do is allow for slightly more than is indicated by the parallax marks. A one-off trial will give you all the information you need. At the same time, don't expect the framing accuracy you get with an SLR, though both SLR and compact usually incorporate a 10 per cent safety margin around the visible part of the image.

Being able to do close-ups with a compact is quite a bonus, but you will not be able to duplicate the modelling and controlled differential focusing you can get with a telephoto on an SLR. With adult portraits, for example, you will find less exaggerated perspective of the features in a profile than in a full-face, and if photographing a child, get down on a level with the face. Pointing the camera downwards at such short distances will give an enormous head and a tiny body as a background.

Finally, remember that depth-of-field is minimal in close-ups and you'll need to stop down to about $f/11$ if your compact is of the manual, or manual override, type. So, when photographing a group of flowers, try to get the principal blooms in the same plane.

13.
All About Flash

The beginner usually thinks of flash photography as a method of taking portrait or record shots indoors, when the available light is poor. The flash is clipped into the camera shoe, and the lighting effect obtained is flat and uninteresting. In fact, even the simplest flashgun is capable of producing far more interesting effects than this. Flash can be used for quite sophisticated lighting, and it can also be used to relieve heavy shadows outdoors under the glare of the sun. This chapter explains the principles behind successful flash photography, and how the amateur can put them into practice.

Guide numbers

The first thing to understand about flash is that it is subject to the inverse square law—double the distance, quadruple the exposure.

Simple flashguns carry a scale showing how the aperture of the lens should be adjusted according to the distance, and every packet of flashbulbs and flashcubes has a table of apertures and shutter speeds applicable at various distances. These are related to the speed of the film.

The power of a flash is expressed as a guide number (GN), which the manufacturer may give in feet or metres, or

This was taken by bounce-flash, with a powerful flashgun aimed at the ceiling. The separate computer sensor on the camera remains aimed at the subject, to give correct exposure.

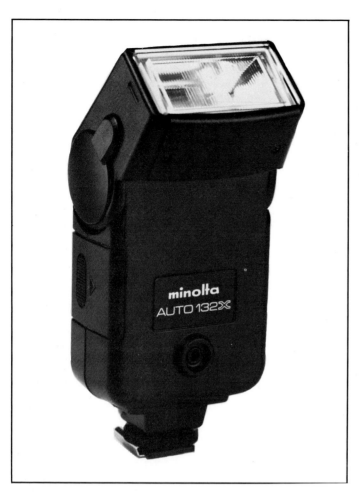

A modern flashgun with a tilting head for bouncing the flash from wall or ceiling. The sensor for giving the correct exposure automatically can be seen on the front. The unit also has a tester (flash distance checker) which lights if the flash is strong enough for the shot.

by the distance at the foot of its column. For example, for 80–125 ASA film, we have approximate guide numbers of GN43 (feet) and GN13 (metres).

Bulb or electronic?

When a flashbulb, flashcube or Magicube is fired, the glowing filament or spark ignites the flammable material, usually hydrolanium wire, which burns progressively from the centre outwards. Thus, the light emitted grows stronger until it reaches a peak, then dies away. This peak is not sharp, but levels out like a plateau, and is the part which provides the usable exposure. This lasts about 1/50sec, fast enough for portraits, groups, and so on, but not fast enough to stop any appreciable amount of action.

On simple cameras, the shutter opens as the flash is fired, and closes at the end of the peak, an open-shut time of about 1/40sec. On more sophisticated cameras, the shutter can be synchronised at faster speeds, slicing out just part of the flash peak, or plateau. Flashcubes are intended for simpler cameras, but on every packet of flashbulbs you will find a table giving the shutter speed and aperture settings at various distances. As will be explained in the next section, *Synchronisation*, this facility is limited to certain types of shutter.

Electronic flash works differently. When fired, the peak is reached virtually immediately, and falls away just as fast. Depending on the type of electronic unit, the peak can be anything from about 1/500sec to 1/25,000sec. Naturally, this is capable of freezing more action than a flashbulb. The electronic unit is powered by disposable or rechargeable batteries, and will give anything from 30–40 to several hundred flashes per charge. Thus, it is far more economical and convenient than bulb flash, where you get one exposure per bulb. A small and simple electronic unit can cost very little more than a bulb flashgun. The more powerful and sophisticated electronic units cost almost as much as a camera, so you have to equate cost against the number of flash pictures you wish to take, plus the flash power you will require. Having read this chapter, you will be able to make this decision easily.

Synchronisation

Basically, there are two types of shutter, focal plane and compound. The first

both. To obtain the correct aperture for a given distance, the GN is divided by the distance. Thus, if the GN is given as GN110 in feet for 64 ASA, then, with a 64 ASA film at a distance of ten feet the correct aperture will be f/11, i.e., $110 \div 10 = 11$. The equivalent in metres would be $GN33 \div 3 = 11$. Here is a scale from the back of a small, simple electronic flash unit:

20–32	5.6	4	2.8	1.8	1.4
40–64	8	5.6	4	2.8	1.8
'80–125	11	8	5.6	4	2.8
160–250	16	11	8	5.6	4
320–500	22	16	11	8	5.6
feet	4	5	8	11	16
metres	1.2	1.5	2.5	3.5	5

The figures have been rounded out to the nearest full aperture, and the exposures obtained from such a scale are good enough for snapshot work. To find the guide number for this flash unit, run across from the relevant ASA column to any aperture, and multiply this aperture incorporates two spring-loaded blinds which travel across the camera just in front of the film. Between them there is a slot, which allows the image from the lens to fall on the film. If the speed of traverse is, say, 1/100sec and the slot is 1/10 the width of the film, the exposure received by each part of the film will be 1/1000sec. At slower exposures, the slot is much wider than at fast exposures. Because the speed at which the blinds can travel is much slower than the speed of electronic flash, the shutter is synchronised so that the electronic flash fires just as the first blind reaches the end of its traverse. At this point the second blind has not begun its traverse and the film is fully uncovered. This traverse begins immediately after the flash has taken place. Total open-shut time on most SLR and compact cameras is about 1/60sec. In the dim lighting situations which usually call for flash, and at the relatively small lens apertures re-

quired, this open-shut time is too fast for the film to be affected by the weak daylight or interior lighting (ambient light). The effective exposure is from the flash only.

On some cameras, the focal plane blinds run vertically across the narrow width of the film. Thus, having less distance to travel, the open-shut time can be reduced, to about 1/90sec to 1/125sec, depending on the camera. These details are given in the camera's specifications, and the instruction booklet provided for the model.

Most focal plane cameras indicate the fastest permissible speed for electronic flash by means of a lightning symbol, or by colour-coding. If the camera has two coaxial sockets for connecting a flash-cable, one will be marked X for electronic, the other M for flashbulbs. Because the focal plane shutter must remain open longer, during the relatively slow peak of a flashbulb, the open-shut time may be as slow as 1/15sec or 1/30sec. In dim interior lighting, this is usually too fast for the film to be affected. However, if you are working at a distance with a fairly wide lens aperture, there is some risk of obtaining a double image, part of the exposure from the flash, part from the ambient light. This would normally be obvious if there were a fair amount of subject movement.

A compound, or front-lens shutter, consists of a series of spring-loaded blades, opening from the centre outwards to the full circumference of the lens, then closing inwards. Thus, the whole film area is exposed during the open-shut time, unlike the focal plane shutter, where the film is exposed by the traverse of the slot. This means that all shutter speeds, including the fastest, may be used with both electronic flash and flashbulbs. Naturally, this applies only to the more sophisticated types of camera. Front-lens shutters sometimes have both X and M settings. With the former, synchronisation is arranged so that the electronic flash is fired just as the blades are fully open. With the latter, synchronisation is adjusted so that the shutter is fully open during the plateau of the flashbulb, or during part of the plateau with shutter speeds faster than about 1/60sec.

On some auto-only cameras, both shutter speed and aperture are regulated by a single set of blades, but the principle of M-type synchronisation still applies. On these, and some simpler cameras, there is only a single coaxial

A Vivitar 4600 flash used off the camera but still in the dedicated mode, by means of a Vivitar DSC-1 cable.

The Minolta X-700 camera used with its dedicated 360PX flash in the programmed mode, will balance bounce-flash and ambient light. In this case, that included the exterior daylight.

To take a close-up with bounce-flash, it is often better to use a telephoto. Working from a greater distance, the angle of light reflected from the ceiling is less steep, and the shadows less heavy.

socket marked X, indicating a slow open-shut time of about 1/40sec, usable with both electronic flash and flashbulbs. This also applies to cameras which have no coaxial socket, but only a 'hot-shoe'. Here, there is a live connection between a contact in the foot of the flashgun, and another in the camera's accessory shoe. Such fittings have largely been standardised in all modern equipment, but occasionally a particular flash unit may not make proper contact in a particular hot-shoe. This is more likely with older, less standardised equipment. If your camera has a hot-shoe fitting, ensure that it works in conjunction with any flash unit you intend to buy. Always make sure the foot of the unit is fully inserted in the hot-shoe, as a partly-inserted foot may not be making contact.

Off the camera

Flash-on-camera gives flat frontal lighting, devoid of modelling. Figures tend to be joined to the background by an ugly rim of shadow. Faces at the rear of a picture are under-exposed, while those close to the camera are stark white and featureless. Flash-on-camera is perhaps the least artistic form of lighting in photography, and can make promising subject material into the most commonplace snapshot.

To avoid such snapshot effects, the first thing to do is get the flash off the camera, by means of an extension lead, which can be obtained from any photo dealer. For general use, a 3ft lead is ideal, and this can be of the straight or coiled coil type, shown on page 130. You will also see how the camera may be operated with one hand, while the flash is held in the other. Even pressmen prefer to use this technique, with the flash held about 45° to one side, and high. It gives far better modelling and removes the objectionable shadow to one side and below head-and-shoulder level.

If flash is used on the camera at a distance, say, when taking a group, the picture will be characteristically flat and lacking in contrast. The lower the power of the flash, the worse the effect. By removing the flash two or three feet from the camera, the effect is largely overcome. Another advantage is the avoidance of 'red-eye' when using colour film. In dim lighting the eyes tend to dilate, and if the flash is very close to the lens axis, the flash reflects back from the blood vessels at the back of the eye, causing a far from flattering red spot.

Much longer flash extension leads are available. With the flash mounted on a tripod and aimed at the subject, the photographer is then free to move around and change distance from the subject, while the required aperture remains constant. A long flash lead is particularly helpful for bounce-flash.

Bounce-flash

If the flash is directed upwards to the ceiling it is reflected back in diffused form over a wide area, the effect being similar to ordinary room lighting. A secondary advantage is that the required exposure is similar in all parts of the room. Whereas an exposure made by the room lighting would call for a fairly slow shutter speed, and the risk of a blurred image, bounce-flash pictures are characterised by extreme sharpness, even when the subject is moving.

Naturally, when the flash is reflected from the ceiling, or from a wall, a wider aperture is required than for direct flash. For this reason, if you have a very low-powered flash, the technique can only be used with a fast film.

Bounce-flash is as easy as direct flash if you have a computerised electronic unit with a tilt-top reflector, or if the unit is equipped with a separate sensor, both of which will be described in the next section, *Using computer flash.*

How do you arrive at the correct aperture when using an ordinary flash (non-computer) in the bounce-flash mode? In an average room with light-coloured walls and a white ceiling, the aperture should be about two stops more than for direct flash at 10ft. In other words, if f/8 is correct for direct flash at 10ft, you can take bounce-flash pictures at f/4, regardless of the distance of the camera from the subject. In a very large room, or one with a particularly high ceiling, you may have to open the lens a further $\frac{1}{2}$–1 stop. Other factors affecting the exposure would be dark-coloured walls or a smoky ceiling.

To obtain a high degree of accuracy, and particularly if you are using colour film, it is advisable to carry out a simple test first. For this test, choose an 'average' room. This does not have to conform to a given specification, as long as you consider it average. Get a model to stand about nine feet from the flash, direct the flash towards the ceiling at a point a little closer to the flash unit than to the model.

Now take a series of exposures at all apertures marked on the lens. Give the electronic unit time to recharge fully after each flash. When the film is developed, pick the slide or negative which you consider to have the best exposure. This will indicate the aperture for future use, in any similar room. At a later date and in other surroundings, when you are not sure whether the new room reflects more or less light than the average, play safe by taking three exposures; one at the average aperture, one at one stop more, and one at one stop less. One of the three is bound to be correct. This is known as bridging the exposure.

When using colour, remember that the film can pick up a colour cast where the flash reflects from a coloured surface. In most rooms this will not matter, provided the ceiling is white or cream, but be careful not to place the model too close to a deeply-coloured wall, particularly if this is green or blue.

Using computer flash

With a computerised electronic flash unit, you do not have to vary the lens aperture according to the distance. Instead, the unit works out the amount of flash required at any distance, and delivers it automatically. The flash incorporates a sensor, which scans the centre of the subject over a narrow angle, usually 10–15'. The flash is fired and the sensor measures the amount reflected from the subject. When the sensor decides that the film has received enough exposure, it switches off the flash. The fact that all this can take place in a period as short as 1/500sec to 1/25,000sec is just one of the marvels of modern electronics.

In the simpler forms of computer flash, the same amount of flash energy is expended with each exposure. The sensor simply diverts the unwanted part of the flash to a quench-tube inside the body of the unit. In more sophisticated units, unwanted energy is fed back into the capacitor and stored for further use. This type of unit has thyristorised circuitry, and is sometimes labelled rational energy. Either term may be used in the specification.

The smaller computerised units operate in the single-aperture mode. That is, you set the camera to a single aperture for a given ASA rating, and the unit will then deliver the right amount of flash over a given range. At 3ft, the flash speed may

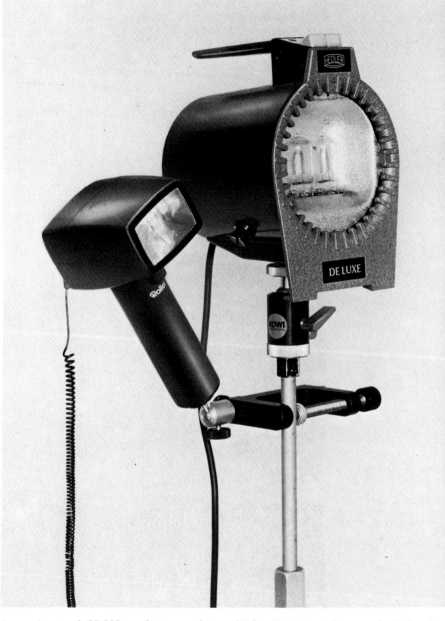

be as short as 1/25,000sec, fast enough to freeze a football being kicked or a dart striking a balloon. The flash speed becomes progressively less fast as the flash-to-subject distance is increased, until the full power of the flash has been reached.

In the larger, more sophisticated units, there is a choice of two, three, or more apertures, depending on the range of distances at which your pictures will be taken. Thus, if all the pictures are to be taken close up you might choose an indicated aperture of f/16, but for middle-distance work you would choose f/8, and f/4 for distance or bounce-flash shooting. The choice ensures adequate flash power in extended situations, and in other situations permits small apertures in the interests of depth-of-field.

Dedicated flash

Some flashguns work in the dedicated mode with cameras which have this facility. Clipping the flash into the camera's shoe automatically sets the shutter to the top synchronising speed, usually 1/60–1/125sec. Then, the TTL-metering combines with the flash to provide a balanced exposure between flash and ambient light.

The Minolta X-700 camera also works with a 280PX or 360PX flashgun in the dedicated mode, when the shutter is set to the programmed (P) mode. The combined flash/ambient light is then metered at the film plane.

Clip-on computer flash units are normally powered by two or four AA batteries, the best for the purpose being the manganese alkaline types, Mallory MN1500 or equivalent. With these, you can expect anything from 100–250 flashes, with a flash re-cycling time of about 8–10sec reducing to 20sec as the

batteries become exhausted. A neon indicates a charge of around 80 per cent, but it is advisable to wait a further few seconds to ensure 100 per cent output. Rechargeable nickel cadmium batteries are also available. With some units, these have to be removed and recharged on a separate charger, while in others the batteries are sealed and the charger built-in.

The charger may be one of two types. The first is trickle-charge, taking about 7-14 hours to recharge fully exhausted batteries. The second operates with special sintered-cell batteries, which

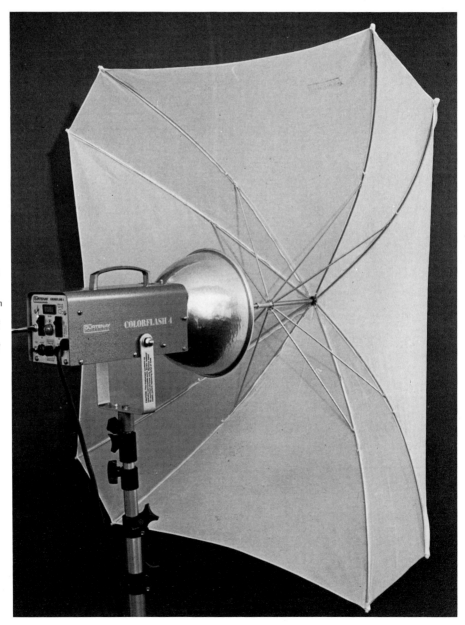

A Courtenay Colorflash 4, with built-in modelling lamp, used with a white nylon diffuser, giving stronger light than when reflected in an opaque umbrella. Within the budget of the amateur, this unit is reliable and will give a variety of effects.

can be fully re-charged in about one hour. Both are satisfactory, but whereas the latter is obviously convenient when a great many flashes need to be taken, the former will hold the charge for a longer period when the flash unit is not in use.

The more sophisticated electronic unit, which expends only the amount of energy needed for each exposure, will deliver many more flashes per charge than quench-tube units, provided all the exposures are not taken at maximum range. Working close-up, re-cycling time is so fast (because so little energy has been expended) that the neon indicator will not go out, and pictures can be taken as fast as you can wind on the film. Thus, the number of exposures possible per set of batteries, or per re-charge,

may run from a few hundred to a thousand or more.

With some units, the reflector may be tilted up for bounce-flash use, while the computer remains scanning the subject. On larger units, the built-in sensor can be overridden by a separate sensor which fits the camera accessory shoe, enabling the flash unit to be placed at a distance and at any angle. One big advantage of working in the bounce-flash mode is that the light covers a greater area, thus permitting the use of wideangle lenses.

Whichever flash unit you buy, read the instructions carefully. Never try to re-charge non-rechargeable batteries, and ensure that the charger is compatible with the rechargeable batteries in use. Mistakes can be dangerous. If your unit is left idle for any considerable time, get in the habit of removing the batteries, to avoid the possibility of corrosion caused by leaks. It is also a good idea to fire off a few flashes once a month, which will reform the capacitor.

Umbrella flash

An umbrella or flash brolly is just what the name implies. The flash is directed at the centre of an umbrella, usually of white or silvered material, and reflected back at the subject in diffused form.

Because the flash umbrella is light and portable, it is justly popular among amateurs, especially for portrait work. The illumination is sufficiently directional to ensure good modelling, but the shadows sufficiently soft to avoid harshness. On the debit side, umbrella flash tends to be rather dull, unless used in conjunction with a secondary, smaller flash, which can be aimed at the background, or placed behind the model to add rim-lighting to the hair (see Chapter Eight). This can be effected by means of a slave unit, a small device that fits the lead of the secondary flash unit. When the main flash is fired, the slave unit responds and triggers the unit to which it is connected.

The small umbrellas and flash units normally used by the amateur, while excellent for head-and-shoulder and half-length portraits, are not suitable for full-length work. The professional uses one or more very large umbrellas, fitted with powerful flash units and modelling lights by means of which the lighting effect can be determined in advance. Silvered reflectors add a trace more sparkle than white ones, and are to be preferred for colour work. A few manufacturers also supply a gold-tinted umbrella, which gives a warm and sunny effect to colour shots.

Studio flash

Many an amateur nowadays owns a medium-power studio unit, like that shown on page 131. Considerably more powerful than a hand-held flash, the studio unit incorporates a modelling light so that the effect may be studied before the flash is fired. Large umbrellas are available for use with such units, the light being adequate for full-length colour work.

The average amateur thinks of his camera as his most costly item of equipment, but for the professional, lighting and darkroom equipment may cost more than his cameras, and are finally responsible for the variety of effects and quality he achieves. The amateur who wants to specialise in high quality work indoors, might well consider the purchase of from one to three medium-power studio units, equipped with slave units, to avoid having connecting cables trailing dangerously across the limited space at his disposal.

Ancillary equipment might include one umbrella, a snoot (which concentrates the light beam to a spot), and a barn-door, which permits the area of light to be shaded on one or more sides, and thus confined to an area of the subject that needs to be accentuated.

When using either studio flash or an ordinary flash unit in conjunction with an umbrella, you cannot use a sensor aimed into the umbrella. This means that a separate sensor must be aimed at the subject, or the exposure determined by other means. There are two ways of doing this. First, by means of a special flash meter, which will measure the flash reflected from the subject, and give you an aperture reading. Second, and without additional expense, by using the relationship between the flash and the modelling lamp.

If you have a studio unit incorporating a modelling lamp, start by taking a series of exposures to determine the correct flash exposure at a given distance. Let us say this happens to be f/11. Now set your ordinary exposure meter, or the camera's built-in meter, to the right ASA rating, take a reading of the subject by the light of the modelling lamp, and see what number of seconds is correct at f/11. Thereafter, at whatever distance the flash unit is placed, and whether used direct, in the umbrella, or in the bounce-flash mode, take your reading, and the correct aperture will be indicated against that same number of seconds.

Even the best flash meter is reckoned accurate enough if the reading is within one-third stop of true, so in many cases you may find that working to the modeller-flash relationship is just as accurate, if not more so. If the flash does not have a built-in modelling lamp, it is possible to use a studio lamp on a stand, later replacing it by the flash unit.

Extension flash

It has already been explained how a number of ancillary flash units can be fired by means of slave units. Some of the bigger, but still portable, two-piece units have provision for an extension flash-head to be connected by cable. The extension contains its own power unit, and has an outlet socket for connection to a further extension head. In this way, three or more extension heads may be used, but there will be a great deal of cable trailing around.

Years ago, many wedding and press photographers preferred working with an extension head to provide side-lighting and avoid the background shadow created by a single flash on the camera. The lighting was rather theatrical in effect, and is seldom used these days. It is useful, however, in certain situations. For example, at outdoor events at night, but even here it is possible to have the second flash operated by a slave unit. In either case, a helper is required, and if people are walking around an extension cable can be dangerous.

Fill-in flash

This is also known as synchro-sunlight. It consists of using flash to lighten shadows, when taking pictures by daylight, especially in bright sun. Dedicated flash does the job for you, but even with manual flash it is easy enough to work out the exposure.

Let us start by imagining that we are taking a portrait in sunlight, and want to fill-in with a manual (non-computer) flash unit. The first thing to remember is that the maker arrives at his guide number (q.v.) in average room conditions, where walls and ceilings act as reflectors. Outdoors, where these reflective surfaces do not exist, the flash-gun's normal settings will result in some under-exposure. This is most noticeable at distances over five feet or so. In other words, outdoors you will need a larger aperture than the flashgun's table indicates for a given distance.

We start by setting the exposure for the daylight, bearing in mind the fastest permissible synchronising speed for the electronic flash. If we have a front-lens shutter we can use any speed, but our focal plane shutter will be limited to 1/60sec or 1/125sec (some have a flash symbol, usually indicating 1/90sec or thereabouts).

Suppose the indication is 1/60sec at f/11 and we are standing ten feet away from our subject. We now refer to the flash unit and find that an aperture of f/8 is required at ten feet. If the daylight were not present, this aperture would give a *half*-exposed frame. This, as we have seen, is because there are no reflective surfaces. If we then expose for the daylight at f/11, the flash will be giving a quarter of the light required for full flash-only exposure. In other words, there will be a 1:4 ratio, which will lighten the shadows nicely, without appreciably affecting the daylight exposure.

For natural effects, we should aim at 1:4 or even 1:8 ratio for fill-in flash.

Suppose the flash is more powerful, and the indication is for f/11 at ten feet. The fill-in ratio would be 1:2, which is too much. This can be reduced by placing a single Man-Size Kleenex tissue over the flash. One thickness of tissue, one stop. Two thicknesses, two stops. It is also possible to reduce the flash power by going back farther from the model, and using a lens of longer focal length.

With computer flash fill-in is far easier. All we have to do is set the flash for a faster film speed than the one in use, and use a smaller aperture than indicated. Bearing in mind that there are no reflective surfaces, and the flash is effectively half as powerful as indoors, doubling the ASA setting on the flash will give a 1:4 fill-in ratio, and quadrupling it will give 1:8. Thus, with a 64 ASA film in use, the 125 ASA setting will give 1:4, while the 250 ASA setting will give 1:8. Just reduce the indicated lens aperture as indicated by these modified figures.

14.
Night-Time

If you want to enjoy your photography to the full, don't put your camera away at night. When daylight is gone, and the lights are switched on in towns and villages, everything is magically transformed. Buildings and streets that might have looked quite ordinary by day, suddenly assume a different character, and good pictures abound. Some pictures can be taken with the hand-held camera, while others require a tripod. The tripod is really the only accessory you need for a whole new world of picture-making.

Exposure

On page 139 there is a table giving exposures for just about anything you may want to photograph at night, indoors or out. In many cases you will be able to use your exposure meter or TTL-metering, but some situations are difficult to assess, and for the beginner at least, the table should provide an effective guide.

Many indoor scenes are fairly evenly lit, and are quite straightforward as far as metering is concerned. Outdoors, things are different. Street lamps and shop windows are very bright, there are large areas of empty shadow, and sometimes there appear to be no middle tones at all. This is where you will find the table handy. It is not drawn from other books, but is based on practical experience over a number of years.

Film

In the early evening, just before the sky has gone quite dark, outdoor scenes still have a trace of daylight in them, even though most of the illumination is artificial. Just half an hour later, there may be no daylight at all. The big question asked by many amateurs is, which sort of colour film is suitable, daylight type or artificial light type?

In fact, acceptable results can be had with daylight type film, but for really serious work I would suggest artificial light type. Provided you work well past the evening, artificial light type film is going to give you the most natural colours, while daylight film will give a much warmer result. Many amateurs will already have a daylight colour film in the camera, and may want to try just a few night-time shots to finish the roll.

In those conditions where a trace of daylight still exists, the daylight film will give just as good a result as artificial light type. The general scene will look quite natural, with lamps and other areas in pools of artificial light looking very warm, or orangy. Later at night, this warmth will cover the whole frame. It is most unpleasant. If you are loaded with artificial light type film, areas which still have a trace of daylight will look quite blue, while artificial light areas will appear quite natural. Later at night, the whole scene will look natural. It really boils down to a matter of taste, and whether you want to go to the expense and trouble of exposing a whole roll of artificial light type film on a single outing.

There are two kinds of slide film balanced for artificial light. Agfachrome 50L, as its name implies, is a 50 ASA emulsion, which is fairly slow. Kodak Ektachrome 160 (160 ASA) is much faster, and 3M's 640T (tungsten) is still faster. If your pictures, or some of them, are going to include faces, there is bound to be a degree of subject movement, and the faster film will score in terms of shorter exposures. It is necessary if you have a fully automatic camera, as a slower ASA rating may be outside the exposure range.

Many pressmen uprate their colour slide film. Ektachrome 160, for example, can be exposed at 320 ASA or even 640 ASA, with very little loss of quality.

There is a slight increase in contrast, but
I have found this beneficial in low-
contrast light situations. Details on uprating Ektachrome film, both artificial
light and daylight types, will be found in
Chapter Nineteen.

Black & white

If a 400 ASA black & white film is carefully
processed, it is excellent for night photography. Even without increasing its
speed, a technique that will be described
in Chapter Seventeen, it is fast enough
for a good deal of hand-held work. For
any reasonable degree of enlargement
its ability to render fine detail is practically
as good as a 125 ASA film. Although
slightly grainier, it is a fact that granularity in the print is far less obvious in
night photography, largely because of
the absence of large mid-tone areas
which are most likely to emphasise
graininess.

If you have aspirations towards truly pictorial effects, overcome any inclination you may have to work the way you would in daytime, without the use of a tripod. True, a fast film does allow you to take many hand-held shots, and this can be ideal for pictures which include people in brightly-lit situations. On the other hand, there are many pictures which can only be taken at slower shutter speeds, or with a time exposure. When it is possible to expose at 1/15sec at f/1.4, there is a temptation to avoid the fag of putting up the tripod. In fact, using the tripod will enable you to stop the lens well down, to obtain much greater depth

To obtain the correct exposure here, the TTL-metering camera was dipped to avoid the direct light of the street lamp.

This table was originally designed for 400ASA daylight colour film, or Ektachrome 160 (tungsten) uprated to 320 ASA. It can be interpolated, and will also serve for black and white.

Subject	400 ASA	320 ASA
Average home interiors	f/2.8 at 1/30	f/2 at 1/30
Brightly lit shop interior	f/4 at 1/60	f/2.8 at 1/60
Floodlit sports	f/2.8 at 1/60	f/2 at 1/60
Neon signs	f/5.6 at 1/30	f/4 at 1/30
Brightly lit stage or boxing ring	f/5.6 at 1/125	f/4 at 1/125
Shop windows	f/4 at 1/60	f/2.8 at 1/60
Fairgrounds	f/8 at 1/125	f/5.6 at 1/125
Brightly lit streets	f/4 at 1/30	f/2.8 at 1/30
Floodlit buildings (white light)	f/2.8 at 1/30	f/2 at 1/30
Floodlit buildings (coloured lights)	f/2 at 1/30	f/1.4 at 1/30

of field, and this may be the deciding pictorial factor. See the photograph on page 138.

Contrast and halation

There was a time when night photography was beset by technical hazards. Uncoated lenses were subject to flare wherever a naked light bulb or street lamp appeared within the frame. Films were thicker, which caused irradiation, and inefficient anti-halation backing caused haloes to appear around every point of light. Apart from that, there was a general tendency to try to achieve soft gradation results with subjects whose charm often lay in their extremes of contrast. Photographers were often advised to give four times the exposure and reduce development by half, to reduce contrast to an acceptable level.

As far as flare, irradiation and halation are concerned, modern cameras and films have reduced these to minimal proportions. Multi-coated lenses seldom flare, and, when they do, the result is usually regarded as a pictorial bonus. Films are thinner and thus sharper, while the anti-halation properties have been vastly improved. In the past, it was commonplace to see rays of light surrounding light bulbs. Today, we have to use a starburst filter to achieve the results our forbears often complained about.

With colour slide film there is less tolerance to high contrast than with black & white film. In night photography especially, it is preferable to expose for the brighter parts of the scene, i.e., those areas near streetlamps and so on, and let the deep shadows remain black and detailless.

With some slide films it is possible to reduce contrast by over-exposing and under-developing, and this technique is explained in Chapter Nineteen. With black & white film we have much more control. We can give more exposure and less development, or we can expose normally and use a compensating developer. Either method will reduce contrast, and both are described in Chapter Seventeen.

Wet pavements or cobbles form wonderful reflectors at night. Not only that, they also add interest to areas that might otherwise be flat and uninteresting. You can get buildings or lamps reflected in pools of water, to add to your composition, and, if the rain is actually falling, the streaks will show up in the more brightly lit parts of your pictures.

Blue sky at night

Have you ever wondered how professionals manage to get that deep, rich blue-black sky effect in their night pictures? It isn't difficult. What you have to do is take the picture in the very late evening, but just before the sky has lost all colour. The exposure is balanced for the main subject matter, but there is just enough light still in the sky to affect the film.

If you live in a town, you will know that a great deal of detail is visible in the brightly-lit squares and main thoroughfares in the late evening. In fact, it is often a surprise to look up and find that the sky is still several shades lighter than the scene below. Naturally, if you exclude the sky, the foreground will still look as though it were illuminated only by artificial light, whereas the traces of remaining daylight are still making a useful contribution. This is a good time for hand-held shots of street scenes, but if the sky is included, it will spoil the night-time effect. Get in the habit of watching the sky darkening, note the point at which it becomes darker than the buildings, but not completely colourless. This is the time for those shots with a trace of colour in the sky. You will be surprised how the colour film can pick out a trace of blue, which may seem non-existent to the eye. Careful timing and discrimination can pay off!

This is a duplicate slide, copied from about half of the original. The original was placed on glass with a light bulb underneath, and the camera loaded with tungsten type film. The duplicate is not more contrasty than the original, as a trace of light was also allowed to fall on the camera side of the original.

Ektachrome 160, which is balanced for tungsten light, was exposed at 640 ASA, and development increased (see Chapters Fifteen and Nineteen). Taken in the principal dancers' dressing room at The Talk of the Town, London.

The dark background would have caused over-exposure of the dancers (photographically speaking!) if the meter indication had been adhered to. Giving one stop less put things right. Ektachrome 160 rated at 640 ASA (see Chapters Fifteen and Nineteen). Taken at The Talk of the Town, London.

15.
Taking Colour

In Chapters Three to Six, various aspects of colour photography were dealt with. The choice of colour films, filters for colour work, colour composition, were all covered. In this chapter we shall discuss further practical and aesthetic aspects of colour.

Colour appreciation

Until a photographer has trained himself to an objective appreciation of the colours around him, it is all too easy to 'see' in clichés. The visual stimulus received by the eye is subject to a good deal of mental interpretation, and even censorship, before a conclusion is reached about that stimulus. The brain contains memories of just about everything we have ever seen and experienced since early childhood, and each new image is subject to many unconscious associations. This is best elucidated by a number of examples.

Ask the average person to describe the colour of a stone wall, and he is likely to answer grey. In fact, if you go close to a stone wall, you will find a great many colours. There may be soft pastel shades of several blues, lavender, rose, green reflections from nearby foliage, as well as patches of brown and green lichen. Similarly, a face may often be described as pink or cream, when in fact it is made up of many hues of yellow, red, blue, brown, white, and even greens. Just try studying the face of a friend—a stranger may think you odd.

A beginner in watercolour painting can sit down to draw a line of poplars receding from foreground to background across the paper. When he comes to applying the colour, he may carefully mix the rich, bluey-grey of the nearest tree, and apply it to the whole line of trees. After all, they are all the same colour, aren't they? In fact, the green becomes weaker, more diluted, as the trees recede. This, of course, is due to aerial haze. The farthest trees may be light grey with a touch of green. This is known as aerial perspective, and is used by artists to suggest distance in a picture.

Similarly, towards nightfall, colours begin to lose their strength. Look at a garden by moonlight and it is difficult to separate the colours of the different flowers, which take on a uniform grey.

The colour photographer should study the objects around him, noting how the colour values change in different lighting conditions. He should note how the actual colours differ from any preconceptions he may have about them. Once this analysis begins, it is surprising how quickly the vision sharpens and the appreciation builds up.

Modifying colour

By means of filters, the colour photographer can alter the mood of his pictures. Many camera users possess only a Skylight filter, which is kept over the lens all the time, or used only under an open blue sky, in the shade, or at high altitudes. That is fine, but there is far more to it.

A pale blue Wratten 82A filter, which the Japanese sometimes designate Morning & Evening, can be used to add a blue mood to a pensive outdoor portrait. When the sun is shining a Wratten 1B or the warmer 81A, which the Japanese call Cloudy, will give extra warmth to pictures symbolising the vivacity of childhood and youth. Used in conjunction with a diffusion (soft focus) screen, an element of romanticism is added.

Colour can be changed completely by using special filters over the lens. These, more fully described in Chapter Four, come in a great variety of colours. The weaker filters used in colour printing can also be used, but the stronger ones should be avoided. In general, avoid green, though cyan and magenta are both excellent for mood studies. Many a superb sunset has been made on colour film with an orange filter intended for black & white photography. There are a number of useful spot filters, by means of which the colour of the central subject is unaltered, but the surroundings become coloured. This adds mood to the environment alone.

Where colour negative film is concerned, or when making positive colour prints direct from transparencies, colour can be modified by selective filtration during enlargement. The control possible by this method is more restricted, however, and the greatest variety of effects is best achieved at the taking stage.

It should also be remembered that one of the most important controls at our disposal, is exposure. Even a third stop extra exposure with slide film will lighten the image, while a third stop less will add depth and brilliance. Seen from a hill or an aircraft, a sparkling, sunlit river winding across a green plain can be turned to a silver snake on a black background, simply by underexposing two or three stops.

Useful stand

Most of us have a favourite slide film which we use most of the time. One photographer prefers the ultra-fine grain of Kodachrome 25, with its superior sharpness, and in return for these qualities is prepared to accept certain limitations and inconveniences – hand-held exposures only when the sun is shining or at large apertures, enough film speed for bounce-flash only with the most powerful flash units, indoor exposures only with a tripod and at slow shutter speeds, and the fact that the film cannot be processed quickly by an independent processing house. Kodak Limited do have an express service for Kodachrome, but, in the United Kingdom at least, there is an extra charge despite the fact that the film was purchased with a pre-paid mailer.

Others will prefer Kodachrome 64, faster and more generally useful, only marginally grainier than Kodachrome 25, but still having to be returned to the manufacturer for processing.

Still other photographers swear by Agfa CT18, a film unsurpassed for its rendering of greens and blues and, at 50 ASA, fast enough for most amateur purposes. It has the advantage that it can be processed at home or by independent processing houses, as well as by Agfa. Agfachrome 50S is the professional version of CT18, but readily obtainable by the amateur, and is bought without a pre-paid mailer for independent processing. Professional mailers for returning Agfachrome to the manufacturer are available at extra cost.

Most slide films are now E-6 compatible. That is, they use the same type of E-6 chemistry originated by Kodak Limited. Thus, they can be processed by independent laboratories, or at home. A easy-to-use and modestly-priced kit is Photo Technology's Chrome-Six.

The new 3M fast colour films, 400 and 1000ASA for daylight and 640ASA for artificial light, are E-6 compatible and can be pushed to even higher speeds by modifying development. It is easy to increase speed in this way, and details are given in Chapter Nineteen.

Choosing the right colour slide film is a matter of balancing your requirements, which include colour, grain and sharpness characteristics, a suitable film speed for your purposes, and whether or not you require fast or uprated processing. Taste plays a large part, and no one film will suit everyone. Some photographers will love the liquid colours of Fujichrome R100, which has the useful speed of 100 ASA and is compatible with Kodak processing, while others may complain that the reds are a bit on the plummy side. Some will prefer Agfachrome. Some are critical of the contrast and relative graininess of Orwochrome, and others love the film precisely because of these qualities. There are also many own-brand films put out by multi-national companies and chain stores, but not manufactured by them. It is known that periodically films of different make are put out under a single own-brand label, so the results may differ. Unless you find an own-brand film to your liking, consistent results of consistently high quality are best ensured by sticking to one of the great names, such as Kodak or Agfa.

Tolerance

Slide film has far less tolerance to exposure errors than black & white, or even colour negative, film. With the latter.

Taken indoors in dim lighting, but a tripod made it possible to expose at 1/15sec at f/5.6 with an 85mm lens. Rolleiflex SL35E, Agfachrome 50S film.

Exposures like this can be made with the camera hand-held, provided a film such as 3M 400 or 640T is used (see Chapters Fifteen and Nineteen).

A black and white print can be treated with one of the readily available sepia toners to produce an old-fashioned effect.

some correction is possible during enlargement. Once the slide film has been processed, however, little can be done to improve the result. Half a stop over-exposure gives too light a slide, with washed-out colours, while a stop under-exposure, though possibly acceptable for magazine reproduction, can spoil the slide for projection purposes. It is therefore important that you become completely confident in the use of your exposure meter or TTL-metering system.

In Chapter Five it was explained that a direct reading of an average subject will suffice most of the time, but occasionally modifications have to be made, especially for backlit or heavily shadowed subjects, or in conditions where only light tones prevail, as in snow scenes.

It is all too easy to override the meter indication in cases where this is not necessary, a mistake made from time to time by even the most experienced photographers. In case of doubt, the advanced worker will hedge his bets by taking one exposure normally, followed by another modified as he thinks fit. Very often, it is the unmodified exposure that comes out best.

Errors are largely due to previous experience of home-processed black & white, and the old advice to expose for the shadows and let the highlights look after themselves, or, 'when in doubt give a little more'. This is the worst possible approach to colour photography, where light middle tones and burnt-out highlights spell failure. Experience is naturally the best guide, but the beginner is well advised to follow the meter ninety-five per cent of the time, making an extra, modified, exposure from time to time.

16.
A Darkroom

Every photographer would like to own a spacious, custom-designed darkroom, but for most amateurs this is not possible. Many have to make do with the bathroom, or at best, a small room with black-out facilities. Some fit themselves into a cupboard under the stairs, or use a corner of the bedroom. Take heart! In my book *Darkroom Techniques* (Fountain Press), I make the point that some of the finest amateur work is produced under make-shift conditions. Provided the equipment is good, the photographer knows exactly what he is doing, and the darkroom really is dark, there is no reason why the amateur should not match the quality of the professional, working in that custom-designed darkroom. Certainly, the professional's darkroom makes it easier to put through a greater number of prints in a shorter time, but this does not concern the amateur, who seldom makes more than a dozen prints in a session.

The requirements for black & white or colour printing are slightly different, in that more equipment is required for the latter. Both require complete darkness, but whereas a chink of light may not affect a black & white print, it will certainly spoil a colour print. The necessary equipment for developing and printing will be described in the next four chapters, but in this short chapter I want to describe the points to consider when setting up your own darkroom. Good planning will pay dividends.

Films

A darkroom is certainly convenient for film processing, but is not essential. A good, large changing bag or a Jobo daylight-loading tank is all that is required.

The changing bag is made from two thicknesses of black plastic or sateen. It has a covered zip through which the roll or cassette of film, the tank, etc., can be introduced, and two elasticated sleeves. With the sleeves pulled up to your forearms, you can safely load the film into the tank in the dark interior.

Inside the changing bag you will need the film, the tank and spiral, and a pair of scissors. The leader of the film will already have been trimmed.

The film is withdrawn from the cassette, snipped free, and wound on the spiral, placed in the tank, and the lid secured. All other steps can be carried out in room lighting. I frequently use a changing bag rather than spend the minute or two required to black out my own darkroom, which also acts as a study.

how much space?

The quick answer is, how much do you have available? For black & white printing, the basic equipment needed is an enlarger, safelight and three dishes. The safelight goes on the wall. If your enlarger has a baseboard about 20×16in and your dishes are for prints up to 10×8in, then a single bench 50×18in will suffice, as prints can be carried to the kitchen or bathroom for washing and drying. A bench height of 2ft 6in is a comfortable working height. To that must be added the height of the enlarger with the head fully raised, which could add another 3ft 6in depending on type and column height, so you may need a minimum ceiling height of 6ft, which could be a critical consideration if the ceiling slopes to the wall.

The ideal amateur darkroom has a dry and a wet bench opposed, a sink with draining board, shelves and storage space. The illustrations on page 147 show what can be done in the average household.

For colour printing, somewhat more space will be needed around the

A hinged board with plastic sheet over the bath, used for contact printing and developing. The enlarger, with electrical connections, should *not* be near water.

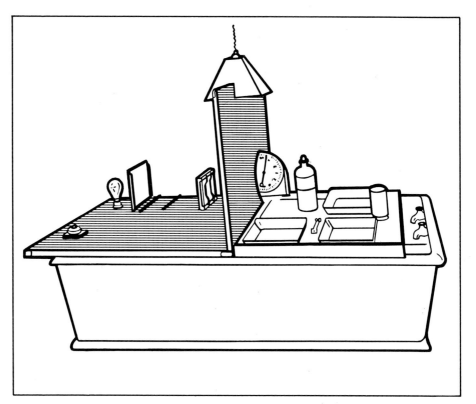

A corner darkroom set up in a spare room. With careful layout, advanced work can be carried out within a space 8ft square.

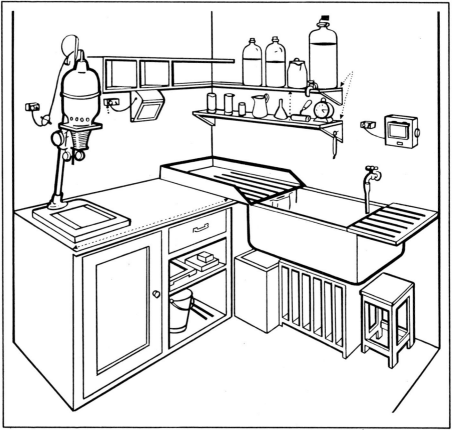

Most of the illustrations for this book were printed here, with dishes on the formica top of the chest. Note the splash protector against the wall. A blackout frame goes over the window.

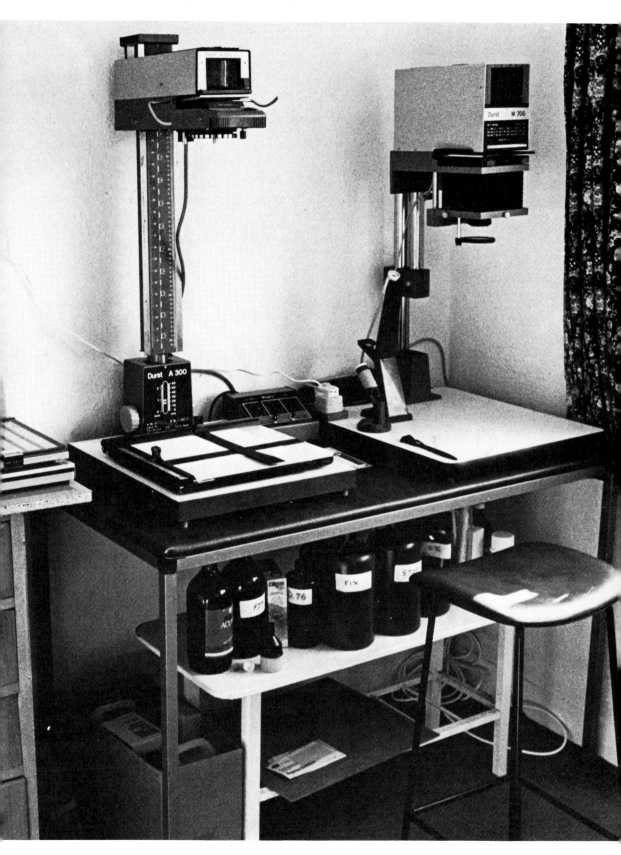

enlarger, for such accessories as filtration and exposure aids, but, as print processing will take place in a tank, less space is needed than for a set of dishes.

Black-out

A large cupboard or closet usually has no window, so black-out is confined to the door. If this is well-fitting, you may need no special black-out. If this is not the case, a strip of draught excluder will do the trick.

A window can be blacked out by means of a roller blind running behind close-fitting wood baffles, or by means of a close-fitting, removable frame. The ordinary roller blinds available at home furnishing stores are perfect, and any handyman can replace the existing blind on the rollers with a length of black-out material. It is even simpler to tack a roll of black-out material at the top of the window frame, where it can be kept rolled up and secured with tapes when not in use. For black-out, it can be dropped, and the edges and bottom pressed back against the window frame with slats of wood. This is even easier, and more convenient, than making up a lift-out frame, especially for large windows.

Black-out material is often seen advertised by mail order, in photo magazines, and a few photo stockists will order it for you. At one time, it was made from densely woven black cloth but in this economy era it is usually heavy gauge plastic. Try experimenting with black plastic garbage sacks. Some of these are really opaque, and a single thickness will suffice. Others look black, but are grey when held up to the light. The sacks can be cut open, overlapped, and stuck together with tape or a suitable glue.

My own darkroom looks over open fields and at night, even with the moon shining, drawing the curtain gives adequate black-out for all black & white purposes, though not for colour. The test for efficient black-out is to stand in the dark for at least two minutes and if, after this accommodation period, you can see your hand in front of your face, it isn't dark enough for colour work.

Ventilation

Ideally, a darkroom should have a ventilator in wall or door. A ventilator, whether of fan-and-baffle, or simply baffle type, is essential if a great amount of time is to be spent in a confined space. True, most amateurs get by with an occasional wild swing or so of the door, but when concentrating on a difficult printing session it is easy to forget—and meanwhile the oxygen is being consumed. That can lead to headaches and worse, so you are strongly advised to install some form of ventilation. A simple baffle of plywood, arranged like two two-pronged forks opposed, and painted black, can easily be fitted into a blackout frame, or a door. A black, open-topped box can also be fitted in front of an existing ventilator grille. It is well worth the trouble.

Extras

Actual darkroom layout is suggested in the illustrations on pages 147–9. However, there are one or two extras, which, if not actually essential, will certainly do a great deal to improve working conditions.

First among these, is a stool which will enable you to sit or lean at bench height. One with a revolving seat is ideal, but any kitchen or bar stool is satisfactory. Although linoleum makes a good floor covering, as splashes are easily mopped up, it tends to be rather hard on the feet, and a ribbed rubber car mat placed in front of the developing bench does a great deal to ease this. Lastly, there's nothing like a bit of music or a chat show to relieve the tedium when making a large number of prints of a straightforward record shot, so a portable radio is to be recommended.

Safelighting

In press darkrooms, a dark green safelight is usually available for the development of panchromatic films. This is not for films exposed by staffmen, which are normally loaded into tanks and given time-and-temperature development. Often, films are brought in from outside sources, and where exposure may have been erratic, it is useful for the processor if he can take a quick peek at the back of the film from time to time, usually after the halfway stage. When the image starts to become visible through the back of the film, development is adjudged to be complete.

For our purposes, such a safelight is unnecessary, as our films will be developed in a tank. What we need is adequate light to carry out black & white printing, and to see our way around the darkroom. In a small darkroom, this can be provided by any of the customary brown-orange safelights. The safelight should be placed so that it gives good light over the developing bench, without too much reaching the enlarger baseboard, as this makes it difficult to focus. In a bigger darkroom, it is best to have two safelights, one giving general illumination, the other placed over the developing bench. The instructions packed with black & white printing papers specify which safelight is suitable, for example, Kodak Safelight Filter OA or OC for all paper-based and resin-coated Kodak materials except Panalure, a panchromatic paper for making black & white prints from colour negatives. This requires a 10H, 10 or 13 safelight filter.

No safelight is completely safe, and prints can become degraded if exposed for too long to safelighting placed too close to the dish. A simple safety test is described in the next chapter. Safelights for colour printing are described in Chapter Twenty.

A ring-around helps you decide the colour of a cast on a colour print, the depth of the cast, and the appropriate filtration to remove it. The dry print and the ring-around should be compared in daylight or bright white light indoors. See Chapter Twenty).

R

R2

C

C2

G

Y2

G2

Y1

G1

STANDARD

B1

M1

B2

M

M2

153

17.
Processing Black & White Films

The basic requirement for processing a black & white film consists of a tank and spiral, a good thermometer, developer, stop-bath, and an acid-fixer containing hardener. Some photographers make use of a water rinse instead of stop-bath, while others harden the film after fixation or dispense with hardener altogether. As we shall see, there is a good reason for following the procedure outlined above. We can start by describing the various items, and then proceed to usage.

Tank and spiral

These are constructed of plastics or stainless steel, either of which is satisfactory, though for colour film processing the better grades of stainless steel should be chosen, as these are more resistant to the chemicals used. Stainless steel tanks particularly suitable for colour, are made by Kindermann, Nikkor, and Brooks. Especially good among plastic tanks are those made by Paterson and Jobo. The spirals are easy to remove, solutions can be poured in and out very quickly, and both are suitable for· inversion agitation. An accessory available with both, is a force-washer, consisting of a tube which attaches to the tap faucet and the port in the tank lid. This makes washing faster and more efficient.

Most, but not all, spirals supplied with plastic tanks, are now made from nylon, and the film is fed into the grooves from the outside. The Paterson has a tooth-and-claw device which advances the film as the two ends of the spiral are turned back and forth. The Jobo has an indented section at each side, so the fingers can feel the edges of the film, and advance them by the same back and forth motion. The two methods work equally well.

Stainless steel spirals load from the centre outwards. The film is clipped to the central core and held slightly curved while the spiral is rotated and the film drawn into the grooves. At one time, stainless steel reels were preferred by many photographers, because the steel wire construction permitted the developer to flow more evenly across the face of the film, whereas the fairly narrow slots in plastic spirals gave some risk of uneven development. In modern plastic or nylon reels, the slots are far more open, and the fault has been virtually eliminated.

Whichever type of tank you buy, read the instructions carefully, and give yourself a training period before loading your first valuable film. If you don't have a waste film, it is well worth using an unexposed one, for initial practice. Stand at a table with the open tank and film before you, and the room lighting on. Close your eyes and start loading the practice film. If the film stops winding, or you feel that it is not engaging the grooves evenly on both sides, stop immediately and open your eyes. You will instantly be able to see the problem, and correct it. Then try again. When you feel quite confident, you can start developing.

Some tanks are provided with a hand loader, which clips to the spiral and guides the film into the grooves, and some photographers find these quite useful. However, any spiral is easily loaded without such an accessory, provided you have a little initial practice.

Developers

There are literally hundreds of branded developers on the market, made by independent companies as well as film manufacturers, and for some of these quite outstanding claims are made. It is also a fact that only twenty or so have been used consistently by a large number of photographers for a decade or

This 35mm Jobo 2000 tank has widely spaced spiral grooves, ensuring an even flow of developer.

This Jobo multiple tank takes five 35mm spirals, or two 120 size.

more. If we were to try evaluating all developers, especially the independents, solely by the claims made for them, we would never be able to decide which to choose.

The types

All developers fall into one of three categories, though some overlap. First, the true fine-grain developer, such as Kodak's Microdol-X and Ilford's Perceptol. Second, the semi-fine-grain types, such as Kodak's D.76 and Ilford's ID.11. Third, the speed-increasing developers such as Ilford's Microphen, though the majority are not supplied by film manufacturers. Whatever the claims made, a few facts remain generally true.

(1) D.76 and ID.11 (the same formula) are the standard by which all others are judged. Among professionals at least, they are the most widely used. They give the best grain/gradation ratio at the nominal speed of the film, as marked on the carton. They are usually the cheapest to buy, and have excellent keeping properties. They are suitable for all films, slow, medium and fast, and are best diluted 1:1 with water, for which instructions are given in the leaflet.

(2) A true fine-grain developer either reduces or limits the clumping of the developing grains, and negatives so developed will stand greater enlargement with less graininess than

155

Measures should be clearly marked and have a good pouring lip.

A narrow-neck thermometer right of page, is useful for checking the temperature of the developer in the tank. Always buy certified thermometers, two at a time for an exact match. When one breaks (they all do) a further one can be matched.

acutance. In fact, most compensating developers have a similar effect.

Part of the popularity of compensating, semi-compensating, and acutance developers, is due to the fact that they employ highly attenuated developing agents and other chemicals which are readily made up into concentrated solutions. A developer bought in a highly

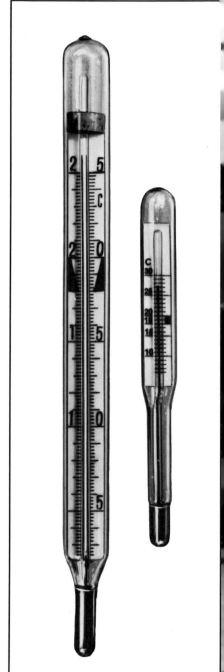

when D.76 is used. This is only obtainable with loss of film speed, usually half to one stop.

(3) A maximum energy developer coaxes the last grain of developable silver out of the emulsion, permitting an increase in film speed, usually one stop before there is significant image deterioration. More developed silver, more graininess.

Thus, if a developer is advertised as giving true fine-grain with increased film speed, take it with a pinch of salt.

Two more developer designations should be mentioned. Compensating, and acutance, developers, both intended for use with slow or medium speed films. A compensating developer has an energetic effect on shadow detail, but retards development of the highlights. It means, in fact, that the developer is compensating for subject contrast. Thus, compensated negatives tend to have a rather compressed range of tones; and are popular with amateurs because they make printing generally easier. An acutance developer uses chemical means to create a barrier between adjacent light and dark tones, giving the effect of extra sharpness, or

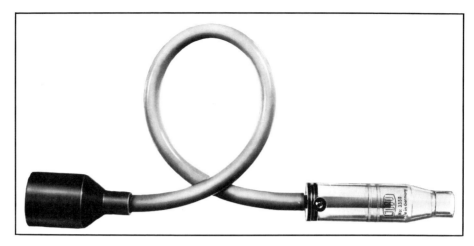

concentrated solution, which is simply mixed one part with nine or more of water, is very convenient, whereas D.76 and other developers have to be made up from powder. This, in fact, is a quick and simple task. A convenient liquid concentrate is Johnsons Unitol. It can be made up at different dilutions, is suitable for all films, slow, medium and fast, and gives results similar to D.76, but slightly sharper.

Stop-bath

This is used to arrest development after the developer has been poured out of the tank, and before the fixing stage. Especially with short developing times, stop-bath is more efficient than a water rinse. The former arrests development the moment it touches the film, the latter doesn't. Every photo store has stocks of stop-bath in concentrated solution. For use, this is diluted according to the instruction, usually one part with forty parts water. Most contain an orange dye indicator, which turns violet (easily seen under safelighting) when the stop-bath has lost its acid strength. Stop-bath is suitable for both films and papers. It is cheap, and should never be overworked. Not only does it arrest development, but it neutralises the alkali of the developer, thus giving longer life to the acid-fixing bath. Half an ounce of 80 per cent acetic acid in 40oz water makes an excellent stop-bath, and in emergencies many a photographer has just shaken a few drops of vinegar into enough water to fill the tank. Why not buy the real thing?

Acid-fixer with hardener

Very few amateurs these days mix up a fixing solution from hypo crystals, which

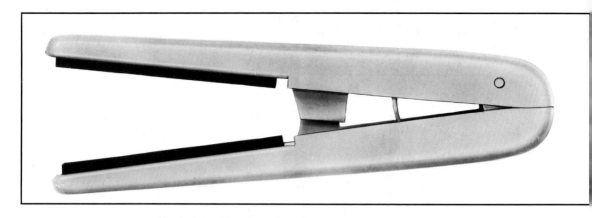

Provided it is kept clean, a rubber-bladed film wiper gives you the cleanest negatives. This presupposes that the final wash water was also clean and free from grit.

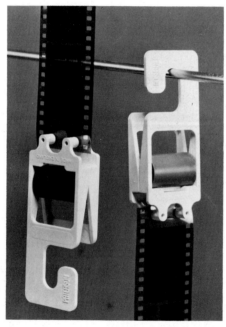

Film clips hold the film taut when drying. These Paterson ones have needle grips, and no part of the emulsion remains wet.

just isn't worth the effort. Many brands of acid-fixing salts, as they are called, can be obtained at photo stores, but read the label first, as the words 'contains hardener' are sometimes absent. This guards against abrasion and scratch marks when the film is taken from the tank, and later, after it is dried.

There are two kinds of fixer, normal and rapid. The former are based on sodium thiosulphate, popularly (and incorrectly) called hyposulphite of soda, hence the abbreviation hypo. Hypo-based fixers are efficient, but take from five to ten minutes to fix fully, depending on the type of film. A slow film has less undeveloped silver to be fixed out, and therefore fixes faster than a fast film. The rapid fixers are usually based on ammonium thiosulphate, and fixation is complete in much shorter times, $1\frac{1}{2}$–3min.

Rapid fixer is more easily washed out of the emulsion. In spite of the fact that fixation can be so fast with a slow film it is advisable to give the longer time indicated, in order to allow the hardener to have its maximum effect. Liquid rapid fixers are often supplied with the hardener in a separate bottle, as it does not mix well in concentrated form. Especially when using fresh rapid fixer, avoid giving much more than the maximum recommended time, as slight bleaching of the negative can result.

Thermometers

Not every thermometer from a given batch will give the same indication +1°F or 0.5°C is not uncommon. For black & white work this is not very important, but for colour it is. Therefore as you will probably be using the same thermometer for colour as well as black & white, make sure you buy a certified thermometer of a well-known make.

It is suggested that you buy two thermometers at the same time, making sure that they are an exact match. However careful you are, thermometers are accident prone, especially after the stores are closed, or on a Sunday. If one breaks, you have the other to turn to, and can later take it to the photo store for matching with a further reserve.

Spirit thermometers are certainly easy to read, but for accuracy mercury is to be preferred. Because of its higher boiling point, this type can be used at higher temperatures, as when mixing developers from powders. If a thermometer is accidentally jarred, so that the column of mercury is broken, this can sometimes be corrected by shaking. A better method is to cause sudden contraction of the mercury by dipping the thermometer into ice water.

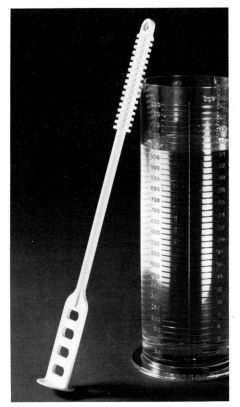

A stirring rod is useful for mixing chemicals. This Paterson model has a flat bottom for crushing the last few grains of powder chemicals.

You should just be able to read type through the densest part of a good black and white negative. If you cannot, the negative is unnecessarily dense.

Provided the room temperature is not significantly lower or higher than the required solution temperature, a final check can be made with the developer in a beaker, just before it is poured into the tank. A big difference in room temperature may cause the temperature within the tank to drop or rise during lengthy processing, and this can seriously affect the progress of development. This is why some photographers prefer a thin thermometer – it can be introduced through the light-tight port of the tank lid to make a check.

Other equipment

All the items discussed so far are basic and essential, but no careful worker would be without a set of three graduated measures, a funnel for returning working solutions to their bottles, a pair of film clips for hanging the film to dry, a darkroom or kitchen clock (wristwatches are too small for accurate observation), and possibly a pair of film wiping tongs with rubber blades.

If your tank holds 9–14oz of solution, three 20oz measures are convenient, and these should have graduations clearly

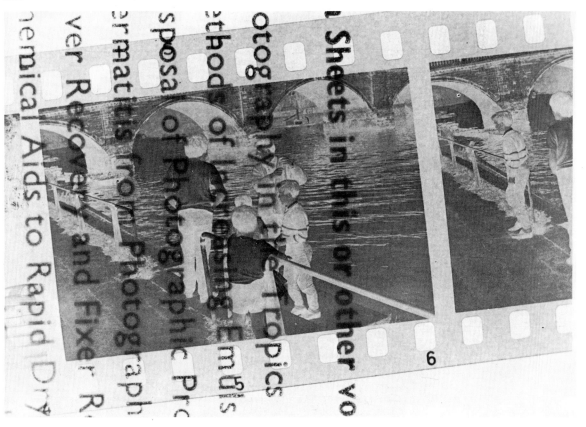

marked. The funnel should be ribbed, to prevent airlocks. Film clips are usually bought in pairs, and some, like the Jobo clips, have one of the two clips weighted with lead. This one goes at the bottom, and keeps the film taut while drying.

Whether or not to use wiper tongs is a matter of opinion, and this will be discussed in a moment, but no-one would argue about the advisability of a good, easily read clock, preferably with a sweep hand. A word of warning – be careful of some small kitchen timers which work by turning the dial against a clockwork spring. Certain makes run down quite fiercely, and the one in our household actually takes only $4\frac{1}{2}$min to complete a marked 5min cycle.

160

Procedure

The following sequence shows, step–by–step, how a film is processed:

(1) With the film in the tank, measure out the right amount of developer, stop-bath and fixer into the three measures. Ensure that the developer is the right temperature.

(2) Pour in the developer and start the clock.

(3) Tap the base of the tank smartly against the bench to dislodge any air bubbles that may have formed on the film. Give initial agitation by inverting the tank, according to the instructions packed with the developer.

(4) Periodically, agitate the tank according to the instructions packed with the developer.

(5) 20–30sec before development is complete, pour out the developer. This will enable you to start pouring in the stop-bath directly the clock indicates full development. Agitate once or twice, for a minute, then pour out the stop-bath.

(6) Pour in the fixer and agitate occasionally, until fixation is complete.

(7) Pour out the fixer and wash the film under running water for ten to fifteen minutes. When using a force-washer, ten minutes is ample, provided the fill-time does not exceed fifteen seconds.

(8) Remove the film from the tank, handling carefully by the ends only, wipe down with the film tongs, and hang up to dry.

Some photographers prefer to give a final rinse in water with a few drops of wetting agent added, then hang the film to drain without wiping down. Later, any drying marks can be removed from the back of the film by gentle rubbing with a well-washed handkerchief. Others give the film a careful wipe down, after hanging, with a wrung-out wad of chamois leather or a viscose sponge of photographic quality. Provided the rubber blades of the film tongs are kept clean and always rinsed after, and just before, use, the danger of scratching is slight. Having wiped down many hundreds of films with tongs for more than a decade, I have never yet had a film scratched by this method, which undoubtedly gives the cleanest result.

The film should be hung to dry in as dustfree an atmosphere as possible, which, in most houses, means the bathroom, where there are less furnishings. Resist the temptation to examine the film closely until it is quite dry, then cut it up, carefully put the strips in a negative sleeve, where they will remain clean and ready for printing.

Taken in dull light, the negative was not particularly sharp. However, the contrast of the two figures gives an appearance of sharpness to the print.

18.
Black and White Printing

In Chapters Sixteen and Seventeen we described how to organise a darkroom, and how to develop black & white films. In this chapter we can run through the equipment and techniques of black & white printing. This is a very large subject, which is covered in depth in my book, *Darkroom Techniques, Fountain Press*.

Here, instructions are given for the production of good 'straight' enlargements, while more advanced techniques, such as pseudo-solarisation, montage and lith printing, are explained in outline.

The enlarger

It is a fact that most amateurs rapidly learn to produce excellent negatives, but find it harder to produce good prints from them. This is sometimes due to shortcomings in the enlarger, sometimes to the technique employed. A good enlarger is in many ways like a good camera. In the camera, the film should be held dead flat on the guide rails, and the lens should be capable of reproducing the scene before it with edge-to-edge sharpnes.. In the enlarger the negative should be held dead flat, and the enlarging lens capable of projecting all the negative detail on to the paper. This ability to project a 'flat field' is even more important in an enlarging lens than it is in a camera lens.

Some enlargers have a negative carrier that is, in effect, a glass sandwich. Others have glassless carriers, and in a few the bottom plano surface of the condenser sits on the negative, holding it flat against a metal cut-out frame. The glass sandwich type works perfectly, but is difficult to keep spotlessly clean, while any small scratch will appear on every print made. Such a carrier can often be modified by removing the bottom sheet of glass, leaving just two surfaces to keep clean. As the negative is inserted emulsion side down, and as any tendency to curl is with the emulsion inwards, the single sheet of glass will hold the negative flat enough for all practical purposes. As the glossy back of the film is in contact with the glass, in a humid atmosphere there is sometimes a problem with Newton's Rings, oyster-shaped markings which appear on the print. If the darkroom is dry and properly ventilated, the enlarger allowed to warm up, and the glass wiped carefully, Newton's Rings can be eliminated without too much trouble.

Glassless carriers do away with the problem of Newton's Rings, but must grip the negative securely along the edges, to prevent buckling. In my own Durst enlargers, I prefer a glassless carrier for 35mm, a glass carrier for 6 x 4.5cm negatives, as the larger negative can buckle more easily.

There is no substitute for a first-class enlarging lens, which will have a minimum of four, and perhaps five or six elements. True, as with a camera lens, stopping down gives extra depth-of-field, and this tends to cover curvature of field, but a good enlarging lens should give a contrasty image, with corner-to-corner sharpness, at wide aperture. Whereas the camera lens is designed to give optimum performance near Infinity, the enlarger lens is designed for the relatively short distances between lens and baseboard. Reversing a camera lens enables it to give a sharper image for extreme close-up work, but you should not be tempted to use your camera lens for enlarging. Apart from possible heat damage, a slight fumble can result in the lens being dropped.

The optical system of the enlarger, which includes the lens, condenser(s) and lamp, must be capable of projecting

Three representative examples of modern enlargers. The Paterson is modestly priced and will cope with most amateur enlarging. It is fitted with a filter drawer. The Durst M305 Color has built-in yellow, magenta and cyan dichroic filtration, but can also be used for black and white. The Beseler 23CII is a rugged and sophisticated instrument for negatives from 110 up to 6x9cm. It can be fitted with a colour head. The Negatrans carrier, seen on the baseboard, has a ratchet for drawing even a single negative accurately across the track.

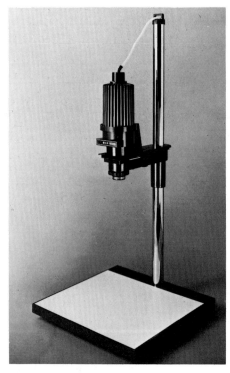

the image with perfectly even illumination. This is more difficult to achieve with a straight-through optical system, where the components share a straight axis than with the reflex systems common to good modern enlargers. In a straight-through enlarger, stopping down the lens does something to make the illumination more even, but seldom achieves the perfect evenness of a good Durst enlarger or similar.

Rigidity is another important factor of a good enlarger. Many of the columns used in amateur enlargers are just not capable of holding the enlarger head without vibration, especially when it is raised near the top of the column. This can be largely negated by having a rubber or wood buffer between the wall and the top of the column. Instructions and specifications for enlargers do not always give the degree of enlargement that can be obtained with a standard lens (50mm for 35mm negatives, 80mm for 6×6cm) with the head fully raised. About 27in clearance, for example, is needed between lens and paper, to make a 20×16in print from a 35mm negative.

Even if you intend to do only black & white enlarging, it is worth buying an enlarger with a colour head, or to which a colour head can be added, as the day may come when you want to try colour printing, or do some for a friend.

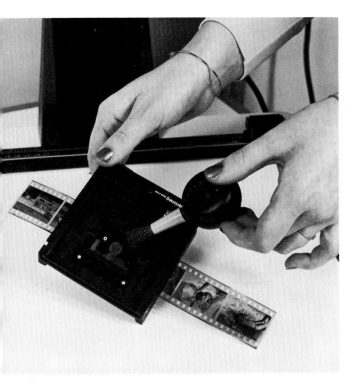

them for pouring out, at which stage they tend to fold and slop the solution out.

The dish is always slightly larger than the size of paper for which it is intended. Naturally, you don't need a set of dishes for every size print you may make. Most of my black & white prints are A4, so I use a set of A4 dishes. I also keep one 7 × 5in dish for occasions when I need to make just a few smaller prints. As the stop-bath and fixer are used repeatedly, and can be returned to their bottles, I use the A4 dishes for these solutions, while the 7 × 5in dish is economical on developer, which I do not save. I also keep a set of three 15 × 12in dishes, and a set for 20 × 16in prints.

Some dishes are supplied in colour-coded sets, presumably to ensure that you don't try to develop in the fixer! In fact, you should always arrange your dishes in the same sequence, left to right or right to left, with the developer dish nearest the enlarger, so white dishes are fine. Personally, I like the clinical look. Tongs are available for lifting prints from dish to dish. They prevent sensitive skins coming in contact with the developer, but some photographers find them awkward to use.

A dusting brush is not only useful for the camera lens. In the darkroom, it can save laborious spotting of prints.

Masking frames

It is advisable to get an adjustable masking frame that will accept A4 paper (21 × 29.7cm). This will do for all prints up to that size, while larger sheets can be held directly on the baseboard with pins or scraps of double-sided adhesive tape at the corners. This is useful, as removal of the masking frame allows a greater distance between lens and paper. A good masking frame allows the margin width to be adjusted up to an inch or more. The arms are usually spring-loaded, and in cheaper models do not always sit dead square. Check this feature if possible before buying.

Dishes

You will need a set of three, for developer, stop-bath and fixer. Although any sort of dish can be used, you are strongly advised to purchase the genuine photographic article. Stainless steel and enamelled iron are still available, and look superb, but tough plastic has now become the order of the day. These dishes have grooved bottoms, to prevent prints 'sticking', and a good pouring lip. With the larger sizes, for 15 × 12in and up, buy only the toughest dishes. Some of the flimsier ones work well until the end of a printing session, when you try to lift

Enlarging paper

In recent years there has been much argument about the relative merits of traditional fibre-based and resin-coated (RC) enlarging materials. In the former, the emulsion is laid on singleweight or doubleweight paper, while in the latter it lies between resin layers. The advantage of RC 'papers' is that solutions reach the emulsion more quickly, and are more easily removed, and they dry flat and quickly. Here are the relative processing and finishing times for the two materials:

	paper	RC
develop	1½–2min	1–1½min
stop-bath	¼min	¼min
fix (rapid type)	5min	2min
wash, running water	30min	4min
dry by hanging, after blotting, approx.	30–60min	6min

If you want to impart a high gloss to singleweight glossy paper, after washing, the paper must be squeegeed in contact with a glazing plate, and dried in a heated press until the paper 'cracks' away from the plate. If the surface of the paper is not to be blemished by speckle, oyster marks or unglazed areas, the procedure has to be carried out with

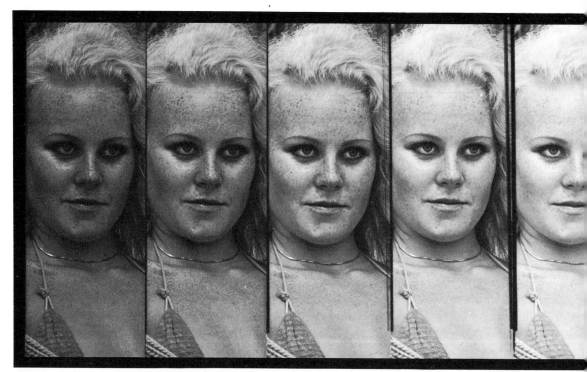

Two kinds of test strip. As the
skin tones were important in
the portrait, the same area was
exposed each time. In the
bridge scene, the paper was
uncovered in steps across the
frame.

meticulous cleanliness and care. Glossy RC paper dries naturally with a high gloss, and with perfect flatness.

Only with the textured papers, such as fine and rough lustre, are there real advantages in using conventional paper. It can be argued that these are aesthetically more pleasing, that richer tones can be obtained, and that the surfaces are easier to scrape with a scalpel for retouching. RC papers are obtainable in less surface varieties, but are so convenient to use that they are now generally accepted by amateur and professional alike. A really good RC print, in any case, leaves little to be desired, and the four surfaces available, glossy, matt, lustre-lux and pearl, cover every requirement. On a practical note, the rationalisation programmes of the big manufacturers are such that the variety of types and surfaces of fibre-based materials have become more and more restricted, and the trend looks like continuing.

Glossy papers of either type are available in five or even six grades of contrast, according to the manufacturer. These range from very soft to soft, normal, contrast (or hard), extra contrasty, and extra extra contrasty. They are usually designated Grades 0, 1, 2, 3, 4, 5. Papers with textured surfaces are often available only in Grades 1, 2 and 3. A soft grade of paper will compensate for a contrasty negative, and *vice versa*, while the majority of negatives can be printed on Grade 2, or normal. Some papers are of variable contrast, such as Ilford Multigrade and Kodak Polycontrast, the degree of contrast being adjusted by a selection of filters, normally placed in a holder beneath the enlarging lens. Most photographers simply dial in the appropriate filter colour by means of the colour head.

Chemicals

Any good paper developer will do the job. Perhaps the most widely used is Kodak D.163, which gives neutral colour and medium to high contrast. Special developers are available which give warmer or colder tones than average, but any standard developer is good to start with.

Many printers use only a water bath between developer and fixer, but a stop-bath has two main advantages. It arrests development instead of merely slowing it down, which is particularly useful if a (*a*) the hand is being used to shade the portrait image, while more exposure is given to darken the background. (*b*) a dodger, simply made from card and thin wire, is used to 'hold back' a face in shadow, while extra exposure is given to the rest of the print. (*c*) Here, the face was too pale, and is being 'burned in' through a hole in a card. Dodgers and masks should be kept moving slightly during exposure, to prevent hard edges.

print has been accidentally over-exposed and has to be 'snatched' from the developer. It neutralises the developer carried over with the paper from the developer dish, preserves the life of the fixing bath, and avoids the risk of yellow stains appearing on the prints.

Fixing baths for papers are less concentrated than those used for films, and can be of the normal or rapid type described in Chapter Seventeen. Dilution instructions are packed with each brand. Paper fixers should contain acid, and preferably hardener. The inclusion of hardener is particularly important with conventional fibre-based glossy materials which will later be heat-glazed, and prevents the frilling of edges in hot weather.

Washing and drying

Enlarging materials should be thoroughly washed before drying, to ensure permanency. An incompletely washed print is liable to fade or stain at a later date. Always follow the instructions supplied with the paper. Washing can be carried out in a dish, by means of a hose arranged to give a circular flow, and if a number of prints are placed face to face, back to back, with the bottom ones occasionally being brought to the top, this method is quite satisfactory. The water can also come direct from the faucet, and if this is pointed down at the pouring lip, the water will be directed across the dish, making for better circulation. Even better, is a properly designed print washer which ensures good circulation and efficient removal of fixer-laden water. Several types are available.

After washing, the prints should be carefully dried. Fibre-based single-weight paper must be dried in a heated press, otherwise it will curl badly. Doubleweight paper can be dried in the press or simply blotted and left face up on dry towelling or newspaper. For glazing, singleweight paper is preferred, as it can more easily be squeegeed in contact with the glazing plate. All other papers are dried face up between press and apron, without the glazing plate.

After blotting or wiping, RC papers can simply be left face up to dry on a towel, or hung by one corner from a line. There are many RC paper driers on the market, ranging from a simple rack (an ordinary record rack does the job) to cabinets with blown air and controlled temperature. If RC prints are dried in a press designed for conventional papers, the lowest heat should be used, and the heat switched off periodically. Too much heat will melt the RC surface.

Safelight tests

Before your first printing session, carry out a simple test to prove that your safelight is really safe. Having set the safelight above the dishes at the distance recommended in the instructions given for the safelight, place a strip of printing paper on the bench with a coin at the centre. Remember, sheets of printing paper may be exposed to safelighting for a minute or more at the enlarger, then for perhaps two-and-a-half minutes while developing and passing through the stop-bath, before reaching the safety of

This Rex-coated cat was posed on a curved sheet of pure white paper. Using a grade 3 paper to show detail in the dark coat has also kept the paper white in printing.

the fixer. Therefore, leave the paper and coin exposed to the safelight for about three minutes before developing it fully, face up in the developer. After fixing, inspect the paper in white light. If the circle of the coin can be seen, the safelight is unsafe, or, much more likely, too close to the dish. Take it farther away and try again. Take into consideration the fact that when developing a print, it can remain face down during the initial stages.

Straight printing

If there is any 'secret' about making a good, straight print, it is simply this: Choose the right grade of paper for the negative, give it just enough enlarging exposure, then develop it fully. Only in this way can you achieve the widest range of tones, and the maximum black, of which the paper is capable. Here is a one-hour printing course for the beginner, though the more advanced worker may also find it a useful refresher exercise.

Start by choosing what you consider an 'average' negative, of normal contrast and density. Focus and compose on the masking frame and stop the lens down a couple of stops. You are going to need a number of test strips, and to be really useful these should be at least half the area of the enlarged image. Half a sheet of 10×8in paper will do, if you are enlarging to 10×8in. A test strip is used to ascertain the right enlarging exposure

The horizontal picture of the old house was printed on grade 2 (Normal) paper, and is of average contrast. The upright view, from a negative on the same roll, was printed on grade 4 (Contrast) paper to emphasise the bleakness.

and is made by uncovering the paper in stages of, say, two seconds each. Thus, a 5-stage test strip will contain exposures of 2, 4, 6, 8 and 10sec. If all the stages are too light, increase the number of seconds for your next strip. After fixing, you can examine the strip by white light and decide which exposure is correct.

1. Having determined the right exposure for your normal grade of paper, make a full-size print. Develop fully. To obtain maximum

black, you may find it best to increase the maker's recommendation by half a minute or so. After fixation, examine by white light. If the print is rich and full of tones, with clean whites and deep blacks, you can be sure your estimation of an 'average' negative was correct.

2. If the best possible print you can make is full of detail but lacking contrast, the grade of paper is too soft for the negative. Make a further test

171

The mucky atmosphere of the sidecar race has been emphasised by printing the negative sandwiched with a Paterson grain screen.

strip on the next contrastier grade of paper (Grade 3, if 2 has been used), ascertain the right exposure, and make another full-sized print. Develop fully.

3. If the first print is too contrasty, repeat the test with the next softer grade of paper (Grade 1, if 2 has been used).

The method can also be used to determine the best grade of paper to be used with a non-average negative. Whatever kind of negative is being printed, and whatever the type and grade of paper, remember that only by giving full development can you get the best possible print. If a print darkens too rapidly and has to be snatched from the developer, the enlarging exposure was too long, and optimum quality cannot be achieved.

A printing session

Start by ensuring that the darkroom and the enlarger are clean, paying particular attention to the enlarger carrier. Have your negatives ready for printing, in their protective sleeves. Personally, I prefer to begin by making a sheet of contact prints as this helps with the job of selecting the right negatives and composing

them on the masking frame.

Place the negative in the carrier, emulsion (dull side) down. Adjust the masking frame for the size of print, set the enlarger head to the right height, focus and compose. Insert the paper in the frame and expose it. Slide the paper face up under the developer with a single motion, and gently rock the dish. One lift every five seconds or so is adequate. As RC papers are fully developed in $1\frac{1}{2}$min, and provided you have proven your safelight, development can proceed with the print face up. If using fibre-based materials, with extra time to obtain the richest black, the paper can be turned face down after the initial insertion, and can stay that way for the first minute. During this period the paper is most sensitive to light, and there is in any case very little to see.

When the print has been fully developed, lift it by one corner, drain it off, and slide it under the surface of the stop-bath. Allow a few seconds, then drain the print and transfer to the fixer. Make absolutely sure that the whole print is below the surface of the fixer and agitate occasionally, say once a minute until fixation is complete. The print is then ready to be washed and dried as described earlier.

Adding emphasis

Even when using a good negative, it may be found that a particular highlight prints totally without detail, or that a sky containing good tone and clouds, comes out far too light. This can be corrected by applying local shading. To bring up detail in a highlight, a sheet of black card with a small hole in it can be used. After the general exposure has been given to the paper, the card is introduced halfway between lens and paper, so that the highlight area receives extra exposure. The card is moved around a little, to prevent a tell-tale vignette. Similarly, a card can be used to shade the foreground while extra exposure is given to the sky. This is best done with the card hovering just above the horizon, otherwise the horizon line will darken in a tell-tale manner. A card can also be used to darken the edges of a print if the marginal areas are too light. This kind of shading is often called 'burning in'.

If a shadow area in the negative contains detail which is lost while printing, this area can be 'held back' by means of a dodger. This is a small piece of black card, or even a scrap of cotton wool, held at the end of a wire. The dodger is used to shade the shadow area during part of the exposure, thus lightening this area on the print. The dodger is moved around slightly and the wire rotated to prevent a tell-tale shadow on the print. Various types of dodger can be bought as a ready-made set, or made up. The illustration (B) on page 168 shows a typical dodger in use.

Other techniques

There are a great many corrective and creative techniques which the amateur can use, and many of these are described in detail in my book *Darkroom Techniques [Fountain Press]*. In this section you can get an idea of what such techniques entail, and decide which you may want to experiment with. Some, like linear correction and intentional distortion, are easy to master and call for no special equipment, while others are more complex. Lith printing, for example, requires special materials.

Linear correction

If you point your camera upward, in order to include the top of a tall building, the verticals will converge on the negative, and of course, on the print. For aesthetic reasons, you may decide that

Photographed in a shop window, this Victorian doll was printed through a Paterson Old Master texture screen.

such convergence is an asset rather than a fault. Regarded aesthetically, strongly converging verticals (or horizontals for that matter) look far better than when the lines converge only slightly, which often has an irritating effect. Converging lines can often be made parallel during enlargement.

The image is first projected on the masking frame. The side of the frame where the lines are widest spaced, such as at the bottom of a building, is then raised and supported on a couple of books. This has the effect of reducing the degree of enlargement at that side, and the lines become parallel. At this stage, the lens is re-focused on the centre of the print. Stopping the lens down as far as it will go, will bring all parts of the print into focus, near enough.

Adding a sky

Sometimes the most attractive landscape is spoiled by a blank, white sky. After the foreground exposure has been given, some improvement can be made by opening the lens wide and giving extra exposure while shading the lower part of the paper with a black card. This will add an all-over tone to the sky area.

It is also possible to add a sky from another negative, and most advanced workers will photograph an attractive cloud formation when they see one, just for this purpose.

The procedure is straightforward. First, the exposure for the foreground is made. If the sky is not dead white, i.e., if it will print with a faint grey tone, keep it blank by shading while the foreground is printed. Next, remove the exposed paper from the printing frame and put it safely in a box, noting which is the top edge. Place a sheet of ordinary typing paper in the frame, switch on again, and use a pencil to trace the horizon line. Now remove the negative from the carrier and replace it with a suitable cloud negative. Compose this so that the sky fits well above the horizon line you have drawn.

Now swing the red filter across the enlarging lens. Replace the exposed print in the frame, hold your card in position to shade off the foreground completely (just above the horizon line is best) and make the exposure for the sky by swinging the red filter aside. You may have to make test strips first, to ascertain the correct exposures for both foreground and sky.

Screens

This is a technique which has found favour with pictorialists in many periods over the last few decades. The print is made through a patterned screen which overlies the image, and effects can be seen on pages 172–173. There is no reason why a sheet of open-weave silk, nylon, or lace, should not be stretched across the print, but it is far easier to sandwich the negative together with a special screen in the carrier. If negative and screen negative are face to face, the screen image will be sharp. If face to back, or back to back, the picture image will be sharper than that of the screen, which may be preferred. Because of the different degrees of enlargement, screens for 6×6cm negatives are usually coarser than those intended for 35mm. For a really coarse effect, especially of exaggerated grain, try cutting down a 6×6cm screen for use with a 35mm negative. Printing through a screen requires more exposure than for a normal print, and instructions are packed with the screens.

Pseudo-solarisation

Photographic solarisation is a partial reversal of some of the tones, caused by brief exposure to light. Originally, it was the negative which was 'flashed' to white light during development, but the process is hard to control, requires a great deal of experiment, and when it fails the negative is a total write-off. Pseudo-solarisation is made by flashing the printing paper to white light for a brief period during development.

The best negative to make a pseudo-solarised print from, is one which has strong contrasts between shadows and highlights, but includes a number of middle tones. Experiments always have to be made, but here is a good initial procedure. First, expose the paper, giving only three-quarters the exposure needed for a full, rich print. Develop the print only half way, i.e., highlights will be blank, middle tones very light, and shadows only grey. Remove the print from the developer and place in a dish of water (not stop-bath). Drain off, and wipe all surplus water from the surface with a towel. Place the print face up on the base-board of the enlarger, remove the negative from the carrier, raise the enlarger head to the top of column and stop the lens down fully. Now switch the enlarger on and off for no more than 1sec. Continue developing the print for the full period of $1\frac{1}{2}$-2min, regardless of the previous time in the developer.

There are two variables which affect a good pseudo-solarisation. One is the stage at which the print is first removed from the developer, which must not be less than half way, but may be longer. The other is the length of time, and brightness of the secondary exposure. Quite a number of variations have been suggested, but the method described is a good starting point for experiment.

Lith printing

This is a popular technique by means of which the mid-tones of the negative can be suppressed to produce an effect like a line drawing. Even the use of the con-trastiest grade of ordinary printing paper will usually not suppress all the mid-tones.

The first step is to make a positive transparency by contact printing the negative on to a strip of special lith film, such as Ilford SP352 or Kodak Kodaline. The lith film is placed face up on a sheet of black card. The negative is placed face down on it, and the two held tightly together by means of a flawless sheet of glass. The exposure can be made under the enlarger, in the same way as des-cribed for pseudo-solarisation (above). According to the materials used, and the brightness of illumination, a trial ex-posure of 3–5sec can be given. These lith films should properly be processed in special lith developer, but a standard print developer will prove satisfactory. You may have to buy a packet of large-sized lith film, but you can always cut off a section. Unless the lith film you choose is panchromatic, which will necessitate the use of a prescribed green safelight, you can develop by the light of your normal safelight. Such films develop very quickly, often in just one or two minutes.

This positive is then similarly con-tacted on to another strip of the same material, which will develop to a high-contrast negative. Finally, trim this piece of film to fit the enlarger carrier, and make a print on a hard grade of paper.

'Bas-relief' prints

These are particularly suitable for sub-jects such as flowers, clearly outlined against a plain background. The original negative is contact printed on a strip of ordinary film, and this is developed to make a positive. Positive and negative are then taped together at one edge, so that the two images are slightly out of register. This particular stage is best carried out on a sheet of glass over a lamp. The sandwich is next placed in the enlarger carrier, and a print can then be made.

The first part of this chapter gave detailed instructions for making good, straightforward black & white prints, and the methods for local shading, 'burning in' and 'holding back', correction of converging verticals, and the printing in of skies, will be readily understood. The more advanced techniques are covered only in outline, as detailed instructions are not within the scope of this book. They can be studied fully in the companion volume I have mentioned. As regards the choice of specific materials for dark-room use, and how best to use them, the amateur does not usually realise how helpful the manufacturers can be. Drop-ping a line to the Technical Services departments of such firms as Ilford and Kodak, explaining a specific problem, will always elicit a helpful reply.

19.
Processing Colour Films

Is home development of colour negative and slide films worth the money, time and effort involved? After all, these are purely mechanical processes. True, there is some excitement when watching a strip of transparencies drying to their true colours, but colour negatives mean little until they are printed. With some slide films, those which can be processed at home, there is the added advantage that you can see the results at the end of a day's shooting. With E-6 films and Agfachrome, however, return-of-mail services are available, and local stations where films can be collected two or three hours after you drop them in.

Economically, there is little to be gained. It works out a bit cheaper to process your own, but this is only the case if you have sufficient exposed films to exhaust the chemicals in just one or two processing sessions.

In spite of these facts, a great many amateurs enjoy processing their own films. There is the sense of personal achievement, which cannot be balanced against financial cost. What is more, modern technology has simplified the job so much that colour negative films can now be processed as easily as black & white, while the development of colour slide films, though involving more steps, calls only for careful adherence to the instructions.

Colour negative

The latest films, including Fujicolor HR and Kodacolor VR, employ an entirely new emulsion technology which makes them sharper and finer grained than their predecessors, and are characterised by light tan masking rather than the former deep orange. Kodak provide a C-41 chemical pack for Kodacolor, which will also handle Kodak Vericolor II Professional films, Type S, and Vericolor II Professional 4107, Type S (35mm and 120-size), as well as Vericolor II Professional, Type L, and Vericolor II Professional 4108, Type L (120-size only).

Kodak's C-41 process calls for seven stages, including four chemical baths, as follows: (1) developer, (2) bleach, (3) first wash, (4) fixer, (5) second wash, (6) stabilizer, (7) drying. The whole process up to the drying stage can be completed in twenty minutes, and the processing can take place in normal room lighting after stage 2. However, the first developer must be maintained at a temperature of $37.8°C \pm 0.2°C$ ($100°F \pm 0.3°F$), which can be daunting for the amateur unless he keeps the tank partly immersed in a large bowl of water at this temperature during stage 1, or owns one of the thermo-controlled processing outfits which are available. Processing is one thing, preparation another. The various chemicals have to be made up, measured out brought up to the right temperature, especially that critical developer, and arranged ready for processing. This can be quite time-consuming.

In fact, independent manufacturers have now produced home-processing kits which do the job cheaper and far more simply, and with fewer stages. Chief among these simplified processes is undoubtedly the British-made Photocolor II outfit, now available world-wide. It consists of only two bottles of liquid concentrates, developer and bleach fix, costs less than the C-41 kit, and handles more films. Both solutions can be re-bottled for further use, and by the addition of an additive, which is supplied, the same solutions can be used for colour papers. Other manufacturers have followed suit.

To prepare Photocolor II chemicals for processing any C-41 compatible film, which means almost any manufacturer's films today, you simply make up the de-

Step 1
Load the tank. Mix the processing solutions and warm them to 38°C (100°F).

Step 2
Preheat the tank 1 minute with water at 40°C (104°F).

Steps 3, 4
Develop $3\frac{1}{4}$ mins at 38°C (100°F). Stop Bath or Water Rinse 30 secs.

Step 5
Bleach Fix 4 mins at 38°C (100°F) or 6 mins for 'Kodacolor' 400.

Step 6
Wash film at least 5 mins at 30°–35°C (86°–95°F), or with repeated changes.

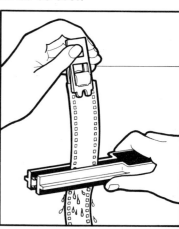

Step 7
Rinse film in water containing wetting agent and dry.

Processing colour negatives is quite simple. Actual times may vary, but this sample is for most C-41 compatible films, using Photocolor II chemistry. The instructions give modified times for individual films. Maintaining temperature and even agitation are simplified by using a thermo-controlled processor such as that shown on page 190.

veloper at a dilution of 1:2, and the bleach/fix at a dilution of 1:1, and prepare a 1 per cent stop-bath, and warm them to 38°C (100°F). In order to ensure that the initial temperature does not drop, the developing tank is first filled with water at 40°C (105°F) to pre-heat, then drained after one minute. From then on, the stages are as follows for most films:

1. Pour in the developer. Agitate for $3\frac{1}{4}$min at 38°C (100°F). A chart is provided in the instructions so that this time can be modified to suit variations in room temperature, which could cause tank temperature to fall.
2. Drain the developer into a measure for re-use. Pour in the stop-bath, agitate for 30sec, then drain.
3. Pour in the bleach/fix. Agitate for 3min, then drain into a measure for re-use.
4. Wash for 5min at 30–35°C (86–95°F), or reduce the temperature gradually to about 20°C (68°F), and wash for 15min.
5. Give a final rinse in water containing wetting agent and hang to dry.

It's as simple as that. Previously, it was necessary to buy separate outfits for processing films and prints. Sometimes an entire kit had to be made up at one time and used within a specified time, which was both inconvenient and wasteful. The Photocolor II chemistry will process both films and prints, and only the required amounts of chemicals are made up for each session. Apart from the colour negative films mentioned, Photocolor II will handle Agfacolor 400 CNS (but not other Agfacolor films, for which other chemical kits are available) and most films packaged for independents. The Photocolor II outfits even contain a 10ml measure for use when adding the colour printing additive, and the instruction booklet is a masterpiece of clarity.

Agfacolor CNS II and CNS 400 have the same fine-grain properties and light tan masking as the suffix II films already mentioned. Agfa-Gevaert supply 1-litre home-processing kits for both; the CN process for CNS II films, and the professional Agfacolor 80S, which is also available to amateurs; the AP70/C41 process for CNS 400 films.

The CN process uses four chemical baths, plus wetting agent, and the steps are as follows: (1) developer, (2) intermediate bath, (3) wash, (4) bleach, (5) wash, (6) fix, (7) wash, rinse with wetting agent, (8) dry.

The AP70/C41 process uses three chemical baths plus wetting agent, and the steps are as follows: (1) developer, (2) bleach, (3) wash, (4) fix, (5) wash, rinse with wetting agent, (6) dry.

As we have seen, Agfacolor CNS 400 can also be processed in Photocolor II chemicals, with only two chemical baths as against four in the CN process. Agfacolor films can also be processed in chemical kits supplied by several independent makers. Neofin Color, for example, which comes from the famous German Tetenal company, will process every available make of colour negative film. For Agfacolor films there are only two chemical steps, and three for all others. Neofin Color is unique in that it provides increased film speed, but it is not so convenient in use as the Photocolor II chemistry.

Colour slide films

In general, the processing of slide film calls for more stages than colour negative, and temperature has to be strictly adhered to, especially in the first developer, if properly-saturated and consistent results are to be obtained. Whereas processing time/temperature errors can be largely compensated for when printing from colour negatives, the positive image of a transparency is obtained by direct reversal, and that's the way it stays.

Kodachrome 25 and 64 entail a very complicated processing procedure, and have to be sent away to Kodak, although franchised processing houses exist in the United States. The results are superb, but this is not the film to be used if you are in a hurry, though an express mail service is available at extra cost (the pre-paid mailer is not deductible). All E-6 compatible films, though, can be processed by many independent processors, or at home. In either case, the film can be uprated or downrated, by modifying the time in the first developer. Kodak will also process Ektachrome films, but only when exposed at their nominal ASA rating.

As with colour negative films, simplified processing packs are available from independent makers, for Ektachrome and every other brand of slide film on the market.

The Kodak E-6 process for Ektachrome films has seven chemical baths and ten stages, as follows: (1) first developer, (2) first wash, (3) reversal bath, (4) colour developer, (5) conditioner, (6) bleach, (7) fixer, (8) final wash, (9) stabilizer, (10) dry. Room lighting may be used after stage 3. Temperature tolerance is negligible for both the first developer and the colour developer, the first being $38.0°C + 0.3°C$ ($100.4°F + 0.5°F$), the latter $38.0°C + 0.6°C$ ($100.4°F + 1.1°F$).

The Photocolor Chrome-Six process for Ektachrome and other E-6 compatible films has reduced the number of chemical baths to four (Kodak E-6, seven) and the overall number of stages to eight, including drying. It is also much cheaper. The process is as follows:

First developer	6min	43°C (110°F)
Wash	2min	34–42°C (93–108°F)
Reversal bath	2min	34–42°C (93–108°F)
Colour developer	6min	38°C (100°F)
Wash	1min	34–42°C (93–108°F)
Bleach/fix	8min	34–42°C (93–108°F)
Wash	4min	34–42°C (93–108°F)
Dry		

One advantage of the Photocolor Chrome-Six kit is that the temperature can be altered for the critical first developer and colour developer over the range 34–42°C (93–108°F), the modified times being given in the instructions. Details are also given for uprating films by increasing the time in the first developer, and these coincide with the instructions given by Kodak for their Ektachrome films.

camera exposure	approx. time in first developer
2 stops under	$11\frac{1}{2}$–12min
1 stop under	8min
normal	6min
1 stop over	4min

When departing from nominal film speed in this way, there will inevitably be changes in contrast and colour, though this is often acceptable. In very contrasty light conditions, for example, you might decide to give a stop extra exposure and reduce the time in the first developer. When it is necessary to shoot action in failing light, you might decide to give shorter exposures and increase the time in the first developer. Reduced development cuts contrast, while increased development increases it. Incidentally, processing instructions alter continually as new films come on the market, so check instructions rather than assuming that the table above is correct for all films.

All slide film processing kits contain corrosive chemicals, and it is important to observe the precautions which are found in the various instruction booklets. Plastic slide reels sometimes become discoloured when used with colour chemicals, but this has no harmful effect.

Stainless steel tanks and reels also become discoloured, and there is also the danger of corrosion, particularly if left in contact with bleach/fix for any length of time. The more expensive stainless steel tanks, such as Kindermann, Nikkor and Brooks, are of a tougher grade of metal and more resistant to corrosion.

In the United Kingdom, the popular 50 ASA Agfa-Gevaert slide film is known as CT18, and is supplied in the familiar blue and red box. In the United States the box colours are the same, but the film is known as Agfachrome. In the United Kingdom, Agfachrome 50S and 50L are the professional versions of CT18, and are packaged in silver boxes. In fact CT18 (process paid) and Agfachrome (process extra) are identically processed in Agfa-Gevaert Process 41 (not C41) chemicals. There are five chemical baths and ten stages, plus an exposure to white light, as follows: (1) first developer, (2) wash, (3) stop-bath, (4) wash, (5) exposure to white light, (6) colour developer (7) wash, (8) bleach, (9) fix, (10) wash and rinse with wetting agent. Dry.

There are independent chemical kits for CT18 and Agfachrome, but none so far that significantly reduces the number of chemicals or stages. Luckily, the Process 41 is supplied in 1-litre kits for home use, and is fairly straightforward. Agfachrome and CT18 are both processed by Agfa-Gevaert processing stations, but only when the film is exposed at the nominal ASA rating. However, there are many independent processing houses which handle this material, and some are prepared to uprate it if requested.

20.
Colour Printing

Because your colour negative has tan or orange masking, it is not easy to analyse, or even recognise, the colours it contains. Basically, each colour in the negative is the complementary of the original colour in the subject. Thus, red appears as green, and green as red. The colour paper used for enlarging from colour negatives has a similar structure, consisting of three emulsion layers, each of which is sensitive to about one-third of the visible spectrum.

To obtain a proper translation from negative to positive, it is necessary that each of these layers receives light of the appropriate colour. This can be done in one of two ways. The first is by making three successive exposures through red, green and blue filters, and is known as additive printing. The second is to make one exposure through a combination of yellow, magenta and cyan filters, and is known as subtractive printing. Additive printing is simple, but there are several disadvantages. The filters are inserted one at a time in a holder beneath the lens, and there is a danger of moving the enlarger as the filters are changed. Also, the three filters must be of high optical quality if all three images are to add up to one sharp one. In general, the additive system has been preferred by the beginner who wants a modest initial expenditure on colour printing epuipment, but Minolta have designed a brilliant new enlarger with automatic additive colour head. Sets of additive filters are obtainable from several makers, and come complete with instructions on how to make a simple test strip to ascertain the right exposure through each filter.

However, subtractive printing is the universal method of colour printing, as it affords the greatest control. The filter combination is dialled in above the lens, and does not interfere with the optical quality of the projected image, while the single exposure can be made without the danger of out-of-register images.

Filtration and exposures

Many amateurs use a basic filtration of, say, 40Y 25M (values of 40 yellow, 25 magenta) which they dial-in on the colour head of their enlarger. They then stop down the lens a couple of stops and make several stepped exposures on a single sheet of paper. This test strip is then processed and dried. Then, by comparing the test with one of the ring-arounds shown in any colour printing textbook, or on pages 152–3 of this volume, he can quickly decide on any degree of corrective filtration that may be necessary.

A good colour analyser such as the Durst CM50 is a help if time is an important consideration in your work, but after just one or two printing sessions most amateurs learn to print good colour using the test print method, with very little wastage. Re-calibrating an analyser for each new batch of paper can be a bore.

What I would certainly recommend is cutting down the number of variables which can influence colour balance. For example, wherever possible stick to one film and paper, and one make of chemistry. Use a good Durst or similar enlarger, and keep the same procedures in printing and processing. Chopping and changing is a sure recipe for wastage.

Some people are interested in colour technology, and there are many textbooks which describe this in great detail. In this chapter we shall deal with the practical aspects of colour printing, and it should be stressed that technical knowledge is not essential to the production of good colour prints. Shortly, I will describe the various items you can buy, which simplify filtration and exposure, and save a great deal of time and wastage.

The 'grey dot' method of determining filtration and exposure uses a matrix like this one from Simma-Color. A piece of colour paper is exposed under the matrix, and developed. Correct exposure time is determined by reference to the least visible number on a vertical scale. The most nearly grey dot is then matched on the comparator panel to determine the right filtration. See colour analysis opposite.

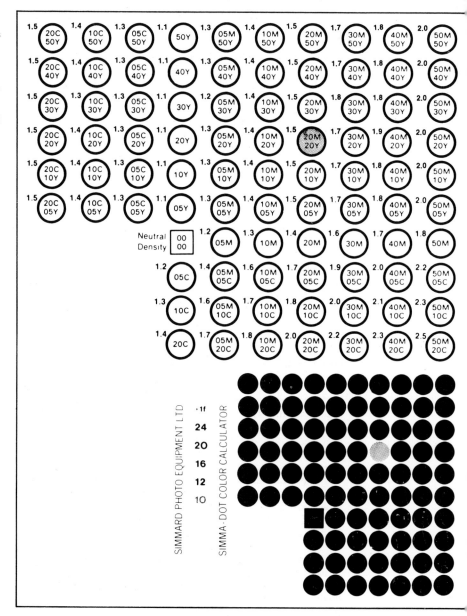

First, we can examine the different systems of filtration.

Filter systems

The colour-mixing head of the modern enlarger is now almost a must for the amateur colour printer, as the user simply dials in any combination of filtration needed. I'll describe the colour-mixing head on the next page. Basically, the requirement is to get the right mix of yellow and magenta, as cyan is used mainly in reversal printing from slides.

Simpler enlargers do not have a colour head. Instead, they incorporate a filter drawer above the negative carrier, into which are placed filters, or foils, which can be bought from manufacturers such as Kodak, Agfa, and independents. Full instructions are provided with each pack.

Filter sets are made up of gelatine foils, plain or mounted between glass plates, though the latter are much more expensive. The best-known gelatine foils are from Kodak and Agfa, the former consisting of seven densities in values 05, 10, 20, 30, 40, 50, 99, plus an additional

182

99. The Kodak CP set has values 025, 05, 10, 20, 30, 40 and 50, plus a UV-absorbing CP 2B filter which is used with all combinations. The nominal density values of Kodak and other American filters do not match those of the Agfa set.

Gelatine filters have to be handled with care, though slight abrasions do not matter, as the filters in a pack are not in focus on the projected image. They do tend to distort under heat, though, and are usually placed in the filter drawer beneath a sheet of heat-absorbing glass (which can also have an effect on filtration).

A far better method of filtration, infinitely quicker and more convenient, is a colour-mixing head on the enlarger. The majority of enlargers sold nowadays incorporate such a head, though on some models the head is supplied as an extra accessory. Simpler, and older, enlargers are designed for black & white printing, and may or may not incorporate a filter drawer.

The colour-mixing head uses a diffused tungsten-halogen lighting system and so-called interference or dichroic filters, and is considered a must by all serious colour printers. The tungsten-halogen lamp does not change in colour temperature or brightness during its life, and there are many advantages to dichroic filters. They have no unwanted absorptions, and thus need appreciably lower exposures than filter packs which absorb light of all colours. They never fade, which cannot be said of gelatine filters. Filter densities are simply dialled in by means of colour-coded control knobs, and as the densities are infinitely variable, precise values can be obtained.

Most colour-mixing heads incorporate a white-light lever, by means of which the filters are swung out of the way for focusing, and can then be slipped back into the optical path without disturbing the combination. The head can also be used in this way for ordinary black & white enlarging.

Colour analysis

A ring-around is shown on pages 152–3. When a test print is compared with the ring-around in good light, you can detect any colour cast which may be present, and apply the indicated filter correction. Some colour systems employ a small matrix, about 5 × 4in, consisting of a number of filter dots, or 'bow-tie' shapes. After the colour negative has been composed and focused on the baseboard, a diffuser, or scrambler, is swung in front of the enlarging lens, and the matrix placed on the baseboard over a sheet of colour enlarging paper, and a test exposure made. When the test print is developed, correct filtration and exposure can be read off by reference to a table. The efficiency of such a matrix depends on the ability of the user to discern the dot or 'bow-tie' which most nearly approaches a neutral grey. Some photographers have no difficulty with this, others do, and I confess I am among the latter.

The matrix can be replaced by a colour analyser. This is an electrically-operated instrument, also used in conjunction with a diffuser. Three colour controls, for yellow, magenta and cyan, are adjusted until the correct densities are indicated. A colour analyser is more accurate than a matrix, and some of the more advanced models also indicate the correct exposure. Such a colour analyser is shown on page 184. The analyser is used in conjunction with an enlarging exposure meter, or a chart, to indicate the correct exposure, which depends on the degree of enlargement, the combined filter densities, and the brightness of the optical system.

Processing, chemicals and paper

The majority of amateurs nowadays use a colour printing paper such as Kodak's Ektacolor 78, for which Kodak supply a 1-litre home-processing kit of Ektaprint 2 chemistry. However, just as with films, other makers have adopted similar emulsions, and this helps towards standardisation.

Although full instructions are packed with the kit, the Ektaprint 2 process consists of four stages: (1) develop, (2) bleach-fix, (3) wash, (4) dry. Agfacolor paper uses Agfa Process 85, which is also available in amateur quantities, but has more stages: (1) develop, (2) stopbath, (3) wash, (4) bleach-fix, (5) wash, (6) final bath, (7) brief wash, (8) dry.

However, more and more amateurs are now processing these and similar papers in economical chemistry marketed by independent firms. These contain fewer chemicals, are more easily prepared, employ a minimum of processing steps, and are more economical. In fact,

Calibrating and using an analyser. (a) Compose and focus. (b) A standard negative is used to programme the filter settings for a particular batch of colour paper. (c) On this analyser, a button is pressed and the lens aperture adjusted until two diodes light together. (d) With a finger on the analyser button, yellow filtration is adjusted until both diodes light again. This is repeated with magenta filtration. (e) The analyser is swung aside, and a diffuser positioned beneath the lens. (f) With the image diffused, a meter is used to determine exposure for the final image. (g) The exposure is made.

The later Durst CN50 analyser also enables you to adjust exposure time when a new negative or different degree of magnification is used.

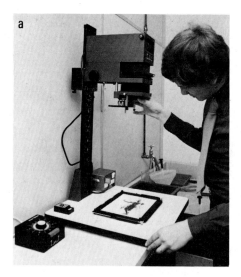

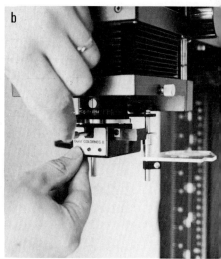

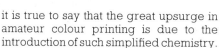

it is true to say that the great upsurge in amateur colour printing is due to the introduction of such simplified chemistry.

The great innovator has been Photo Technology Ltd., of Potters Bar, Hertfordshire, in England, especially with their introduction of Photocolor II chemicals. Just two liquid concentrates are used for processing colour negatives, while the same solutions, plus a small amount of liquid developer additive, are used for papers.

Photocolor II chemicals are designed to process what are sometimes called Type A resin-coated papers, which include Kodak Ektacolor 74RC and 78RC, Agfacolor Type 5 (but not other Agfacolor papers), as well as Photo Technology's own Photocolor RC, and other makes in the Type A category of papers. The Photocolor II system is

particularly economical, as after developing a film, the same chemicals can be used for the enlarging paper. The actual processing stages are: (1) colour developer, (2) stop-bath, (3) bleach-fix (4) wash, (5) dry. Processing a print is completed in about nine minutes. As with all colour processing, temperature in the first solution (developer) is critical, but the undoubted advantage of Photocolor II chemicals is that they are supplied as liquid concentrates, ready for use.

Processing equipment

Color paper is no longer dish processed, as this involves uneconomical quantities of solutions, besides which it is difficult to maintain temperature, and especially to rock the dish in the dark

184

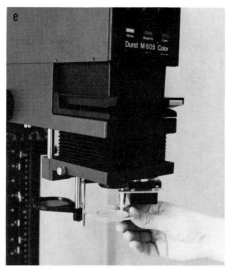

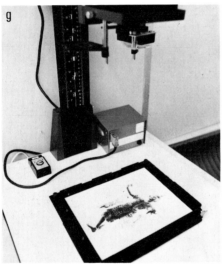

poured through the port and is held in a cup. As the tank is lowered into the horizontal position, the solution flows out onto the surface of the paper, which it covers evenly as the tank is rolled back and forth on the bench, or rotated by means of an automatic or hand roller device. About 85ml of each solution is enough for a 10×8in print.

An accurate, certified thermometer is a must for colour processing. It is best to buy one specifically designed for the job, and the extra cost will be amply repaid in economy of materials.

You will need separate small measures to hold the different solutions.

You will also need some method of maintaining the made-up solutions at the right temperature, preparatory to, and during, processing. A makeshift is to half-immerse bottles of solution in a water jacket. This can be six inches of water in a washing-up bowl, with the temperature maintained by an occasional infusion from the hot tap or a kettle. The method works, but needs care. It can take twenty minutes or more for the solutions in the bottles to achieve the same temperature as the water jacket, and the temperature can drop when the solutions are poured into the small measures. Usually the small measures will not remain upright in the washing-up bowl if the water is deep enough to ensure a steady temperature.

It is far better to use thermostatic control. On pages 188-9 an old but efficient Jobo tempering box is being used. This is simply a plastic bowl with lid, holding bottles and beakers of chemicals. The bowl contains water, an immersion heater, and a thermostatic

without slopping over. Practically every one now has a colour processing drum which uses extremely small quantities of solutions, and which, after loading, enables you to work in room lighting. The saving in chemicals and paper will pay for the drum after just one or two printing sessions.

A drum for colour paper, as you can see on page 188, is basically an elongated version of the film processing tank, but without a spiral inside. The paper is inserted face inward, and follows the curve of the drum. Clips or other holders are incorporated, to hold small prints and test strips in place. After loading the exposed paper in darkness, the cap is put on, and solutions are then poured in and out through a light-tight port. In the best-designed tanks, you start with the tank held vertically. The solution is

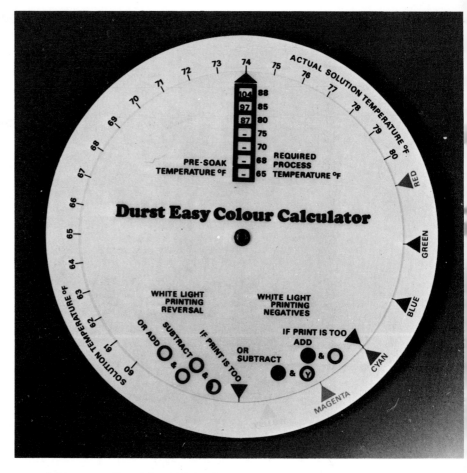

The Durst Easy Colour Calculator has three functions. For negative printing, an index is turned to the colour of the cast (shown as coloured triangles) and the appropriate filter colours are indicated by spots. It will perform the same function when printing on reversal paper from colour slides. Turn another index to the actual solution temperature, and you can read off the appropriate pre-soak temperature for the drum against the required processing temperature.

control. Many people get by with bottles and beakers standing in a washing-up bowl, and keep the water (known as a water jacket) at the right temperature of 38°C (100°F) or whatever, with occasional topping up from a kettle. With a little practice, the method works.

Far superior, though, is the thermo-controlled processor seen on page 190, which also rotates the drum. Many amateurs now use these for all film and paper processing.

Safelights are available for colour paper, such as the Kodak Safelight Filter No. 13, the Agfa Safelight Screen 08, the deep-green filter incorporated in the Durst darkroom lamp, and several others. When first you switch on one of these safelights you see hardly anything, but after a minute you'll be able to see clearly enough to check which side of the printing paper is which, and where the enlarger controls and the processing drum are located. Whichever make of safelight, follow the maker's recommendations with regard to suitability for the type paper you are using.

A useful gadget is a test print maker, such as the Durst Comask. This is a printing frame taking a 10×8in sheet of colour paper, which can be uncovered a section at a time, allowing four different test exposures to be developed as a single sheet. All four covers can be swung aside for a 10×8in enlargement, or just two for an 8×5in print.

Resin-coated paper can be dried simply by wiping off the surface moisture and hanging by one corner from a line, or by laying each sheet face up on an absorbent surface, such as a towel or several thicknesses of newspaper. The blotted sheets may also be arranged in a frame such as those designed for holding records. The job is speeded up by the use of a proper RC-paper dryer, in which the sheets are placed on racks and subjected to a flow of warm air. The Durst FRC 400 dryer has two-element temperature control, and a wringer to remove excess water before prints are placed on the racks.

With care, a dryer intended for black

186

Having made a good print, you may wish to make another of a different size. This calculator works out the exposure adjustment for you.

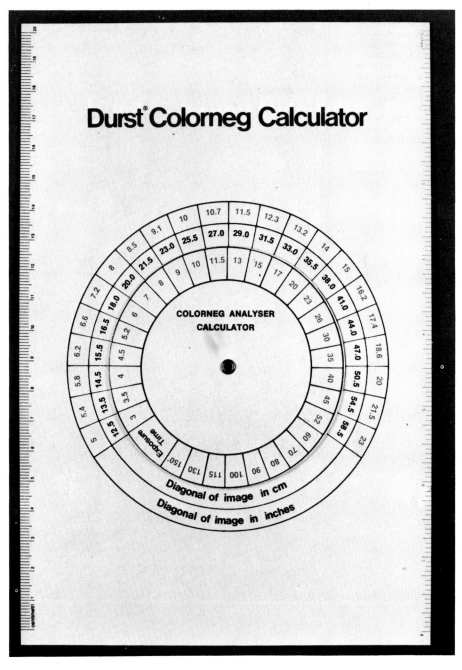

Durst® Colorneg Calculator

COLORNEG ANALYSER CALCULATOR

Exposure Time

Diagonal of image in cm
Diagonal of image in inches

& white papers of the conventional fibre-based type can also be used for drying RC colour papers. If the dryer has thermostatic control, this must be set for the lowest heat and, if not, the dryer will have to be switched off at short intervals. Too much heat will melt the resin coating of the paper. Remove the print from time to time, so that moisture can escape from the underside, then replace for a further period.

Some RC papers are provided in just two surface varieties, glossy and matt. Kodak RC colour paper can be had in glossy, smooth lustre, silk and lustre-luxe.

Making a print

Having read through the previous sections, you will now have a general idea of the kind of colour enlarging and processing equipment you want, both in terms of cost and facility. It is not my

Developing a colour print.
Chemicals are kept at the right
temperature in a
thermostatically-controlled
water jacket. (a) In the dark,
the exposed paper is loaded
into the drum and a pre-soak
given to adjust drum
temperature. (b) The developer
is poured in. (c) The drum is
rolled back and forth on a flat
surface during the development
period. (d) The developer is
poured out, and several
changes of water are
introduced. (e) The bleach-fix is
poured in, and (f) the drum is
again rolled. (g) The bleach-fix
is poured out. (h) The print
may be removed for washing,
freeing the drum for further
use, use throwaway paper
towels, which avoids a build-up
of chemical deposits. (j) The
print is gently wiped or blotted,
and (k) air dried.

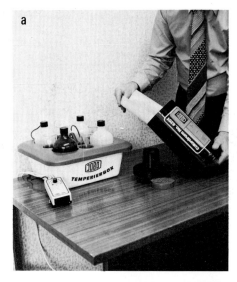

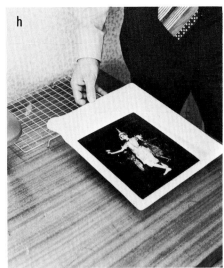

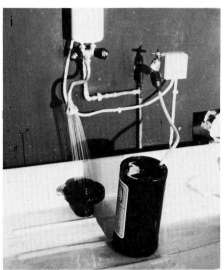

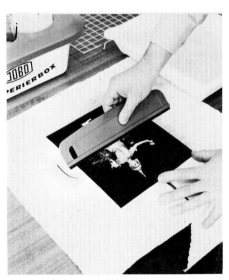

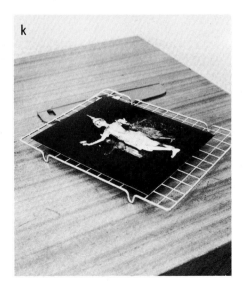

intention, nor is it within the scope of a single volume, to describe the various enlarging and processing methods in detail, and in any case these matters are described in the instruction manuals issued with equipment and materials. It will be useful, however, to describe a typical printing session with colour negatives. Prints can also be made direct from colour slides, and this will be dealt with later.

Setting up

The merest chink of light in the darkroom can cause a colour cast. In other words, your working area must be completely dark. Get in the habit of having everything in a fixed position, so that you rapidly learn where everything is in the

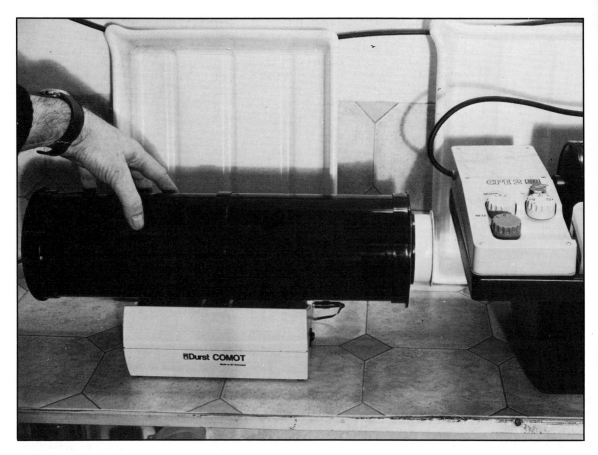

The Jobo CPE 2 processor at right will keep all solutions at the right temperature, and roll a drum big enough for 12x16in paper. Here, the CPE 2 is used only for temperature control of chemistry, while a long tank holding 16x20in paper is rolled automatically on a Durst Comot motorised base.

dark. Once you have had some experience, you may have the processing solutions ready for the first test print, but this is not necessary.

The test print

Dust off the negative and place it in the carrier. Compose and focus on the masking frame. Use one of the methods or devices described to ascertain filtration and exposure. Your test strip can be based on the basic filter pack for your standard negative, a matrix of dots or 'bow-ties' (Simma-Color, Uni-color, Beseler, etc), a colour analyser and enlarging exposure meter, or an instrument which combines both functions. Make the test exposure and place the test strip in a light-tight drawer or box, or insert directly into the drum.

Process print

Prepare measured quantities of processing solutions and bring to the correct temperature. With most drums, instructions are given on pre-heating with water, according to the ambient tempera-

ture in the room. Follow the instructions for processing, then dry the print. A print will change colour as it dries, so it is best to dry it and examine it in bright light before deciding on corrective filtration.

Corrective filtration

The most useful way to detect a colour cast is by comparison with a ringaround. Another method is to examine the print with various CP filters held to the eye. The complementary value of the filter that corrects most satisfactorily, is added to the filter pack in the enlarger. Usually, the filters will only be available if you are working with filter drawer rather than a colour-mixing head. If the filtration for your test print was decided by means of a colour analyser, it is probable that only a small change in filter values will be required, if at all.

Exposure correction

Determining the correct exposure is less of a problem than obtaining correct filtration. If you rely on experience alone, you will be guessing how much more or less exposure the final print requires. The matrix method provides the corrective exposure if the filter pack densities have to be altered. If you have a colour analyser and enlarging exposure meter, or an instrument that combines the two functions, and provided this has been calibrated for the batch of colour paper in use, the test print exposure should be near enough correct. It will then be easy to decide what small percentage more or less exposure is needed, if any.

The finished print

The filtration is corrected, either by adjusting the controls on the colour-mixing head, or by altering values in the filter pack. Then, emulsion side up (!) a sheet of colour paper is placed in the masking frame, and the exposure made. Still in safe lighting, the print is placed in the drum, the light-tight cap is put on, and – *after checking that the packet of paper is properly closed* – the lights can be switched on. The paper is then processed, as before.

A printing frame such as the Durst Comask is a great aid if you wish to make four 5 × 4in prints at one time on a single sheet of 10 × 8in paper, which saves repeated processing. A 10 × 8in drum is best to start with, but much bigger drums are available for processing very large prints.

Prints from slides

Two types of resin-coated paper are generally available to the amateur for making reversal colour prints direct from colour slides. These are Kodak Ektachrome 14RC, and Cibachrome. The Kodak chemicals for Ektachrome 14RC are the Ektaprint R41 process. As with negative - positive processing, Photo Technology have produced an economical kit of Photochrome R chemistry for Ektachrome 14RC, which reduces the number of steps from eleven to eight, including drying. The stages for Cibachrome processing are: (1) Develop, (2) bleach, (3) fix, (4) wash, (5) dry.

Both papers will produce excellent prints, but Cibachrome is noted for extreme sharpness, excellent whites, and non-fade dyes. On the debit side, Cibachrome is a rather contrasty paper. Ektachrome prints, like most colour materials, should not be exposed regularly to daylight, and particularly sunlight. However, fading of the dye images can be considerably retarded by spraying the print with one of the UV-absorbing aerosols which are available. Both papers are considerably more costly than those used for negative-positive processes.

These reversal papers are of great benefit to those photographers who work mainly for reproduction and projection, and must therefore use transparency film in the camera. A well-made print from a sharp, fully-saturated transpar-

The Durst FRC400 dryer for resin-coated paper. Wet prints are passed through the rollers and placed on the racks. Air is blown through at low or high temperature. Up to eight 11 x 8in prints or smaller-sized multiples, can be dried at one time, in about 3–4min.

ency should be in no way inferior to one made from a negative, and, in fact, a Cibachrome print may be sharper. As full instructions for use are given with both paper and chemical kits, I will not repeat them here. Suffice it to say that Photo Technology have again been first in the field with their 1-litre kit of solutions for Ektachrome 14RC paper, under the name Photochrome R. Previously, reversal paper had to be exposed to light between first developer and colour developer, but this is unnecessary with Photochrome R as reversal is effected chemically. The instruction booklet supplied with Photochrome R chemicals is well written, and contains full instructions for exposure and filtration, as well as processing.

One big advantage of making reversal prints is that you see the picture projected on the printing frame, as it is, and not as a colour-reversed image. This makes filtration far easier. If the image looks too yellow, just reduce yellow filtration until it looks right, and so on.

When enlarging from a colour negative, you can hold back or burn in a particular area, just as with black & white printing. The technique was described in Chapter Eighteen. It is also possible to hold back and burn in with reversal papers, but here the procedure is reversed. To lighten a shadow area you give more exposure, and to obtain more highlight detail you give less exposure. Remember, the image will be reversed during processing.

A complaint which has somewhat unjustly been levelled against Cibachrome paper, is that its fairly high contrast makes it unsuitable for printing from contrasty transparencies. Professionals, in fact, often make silver masks to compensate for this. A silver mask is a very thin black & white negative, usually containing only shadow detail. This is sandwiched in exact register with the transparency, and has the effect of reducing contrast. In fact, the amateur will find it quite easy to reduce the contrast of Cibachrome, simply by reducing the time in the developer. This is normally two minutes, but it can be reduced by as much as half a minute. Naturally, a little extra enlarging exposure must be given to maintain density, but the exposure tolerance of Cibachrome is so remarkable that this is no problem. For example, if a test print showed a correct exposure of thirty seconds, and it was decided to reduce development by half a minute, the exposure could be increased by ten to fifteen seconds.

21.
Projection

If the possession of a top-class projector automatically ensured a top-class show, we would all be first-rate showmen. The fact that we have all had to sit through excruciating performances, bored out of our tiny minds by puerile bouts of humour, proves otherwise. So many good photographers, having learned to produce excellent slides, fail dismally when it comes to entertaining family and friends with a slide show, simply because the technique is not understood. The fact is, a good slide show depends on three things – the interest inherent in the material, the way the material is presented, and the equipment used to present it.

In this chapter we will examine the kinds of projector available, from the simplest to the most sophisticated, and, even more important, describe how you can put your slides together with music and commentary to produce a professional-style show. It is important to relate the equipment used to the kind of show intended. If you want to show your friends a series of slides with straightforward commentary on 'My Holiday', a multi-image audio-visual would be gilding the lily. On the other hand, you cannot produce a highly complicated, creative admixture of images and sound on a simple projector with a push-pull carrier.

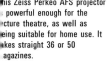
This Zeiss Perkeo AFS projector is powerful enough for the picture theatre, as well as being suitable for home use. It takes straight 36 or 50 magazines.

Two 250W Zeiss projectors used on a twinning stand for an audio-visual show. The Zeiss Softmatic dissolve unit in front is used to fade one slide into another, manually, or by means of a pulsed tape.

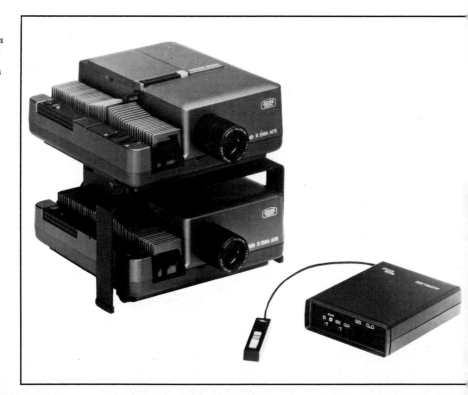

For audio-visual presentations, professionals prefer the Kodak Carousel S-AV2020, two of which are shown in tandem.

The author with an outfit used for audio-visual presentations. Left to right, are a Superscope stereo cassette recorder, two Zeiss projectors converted for use with, right, an Imatronic SX2500 programmer.

It's horses for courses. First, then, the equipment. After that, the techniques of presentation, the professionalism that turns ughs into ahs!

Equipment

The simplest form of projector, though there aren't many left on the market, has a low-powered tungsten lamp, simple baffle ventilation, and a push-pull carrier. You insert a slide and push it into the gate. The carrier now projects at the other side, ready to receive another slide. When this is pushed into the gate, the first slide can be replaced by another. Although such a projector is fine for examining slides at home, the image is none too bright, and the lack of automation precludes any attempt at a polished slide show.

Semi-automatic

The most widely sold projectors are the semi-automatic variety. These are usually fitted with a 150w 24v halogen lamp, an efficient parabolic reflector, condensers to concentrate the light, and a heat-absorbing glass to prevent your slides frying. An impeller fan is incorporated, to blow cooling air across the gate and the lamp, the heated air then escaping through baffles. Not all baffles are equally good. A few models permit beams of light to reach the ceiling or walls, and in a small room this can dim the screen image. If you get the chance, have the intended purchase switched on in the store, so you can compare the baffling with that of other models.

This type usually accepts straight 36- or 50-slide magazines and has a remote control unit on a (far too short) extension cord, which will not allow you to get in front of the audience while projecting. Depending on design, but not always on price, the remote control unit will have buttons for forward and backward movement of the slides, which change automatically as a button is pressed. Sometimes there is just one button, and a forward/backward switch.

Not every projector of this type has the forward/backward controls duplicated on the body of the machine, but this is not really important. By using the remote control unit, you avoid touching the projector, and possibly causing screen waver, especially if the projection stand is not rigid. Some units have an on/off switch, the fan starting to operate as the mains lead is plugged in. However, there is always a separate switch for the lamp.

Perhaps the most useful feature of a semi-automatic projector is the inclusion of a remote control focusing device normally placed beneath the other buttons on the hand unit. The first slide is focused by moving the lens manually. Thereafter, if a slide buckles, or a mount of different thickness is inserted in the gate, you press the remote focusing button which causes a servo motor to move the lens, or the slide itself, into focus.

If you are thinking of adding music, or other sound, by synchronisation, ensure that there is a remote control lead socket on the machine, as it is through this that synchronisation will be effected. Some models have the remote control unit wired directly into the circuit, without plug or socket. A-V linkages will be described shortly.

Magazines

For most amateur purposes, a straight-50 magazine is adequate, but there are certain advantages to rotary types which will take 80 or 120 slides. This may avoid the necessity of changing magazines during a single-projector show. With two projectors in tandem, however, two straight-50 magazines hold enough slides for a 7–15min sequence at normal projection rate.

Fully automatic

These projectors differ from semi-automatic types in two important respects. First, they can bring an out-of-focus slide back into focus without the assistance of the operator. This apparent miracle is achieved by means of a scanning ray directed at the surface of the slide in the gate. If the slide pops out of the plane of sharp focus, a servo motor snaps into action, and stops when the scanner is once more properly aligned. This feature is invaluable if a great many slides in different types of mount are to be shown, and also if the projectionist wants to concentrate fully on his commentary.

For audio-visual shows, some experts prefer semi-automatic projectors. If all the mounts are glazed and of the same

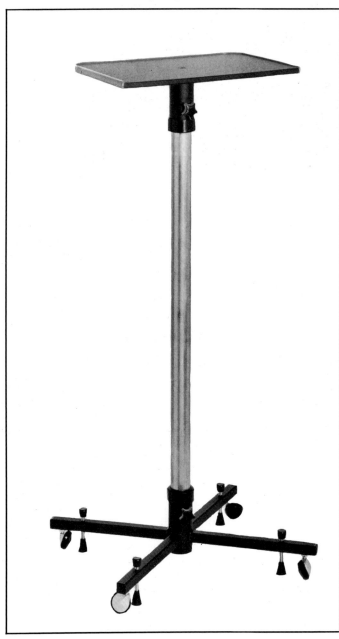

The projector stand is important, and a shaky one can spoil a slide show. This is the very strong Unicol stand, one of a large range.

GePe glazed slide mounts are among the best, and most convenient. For really clean slide mounting, useful tools include chamois, dusting brush, and an aerosol air jet.

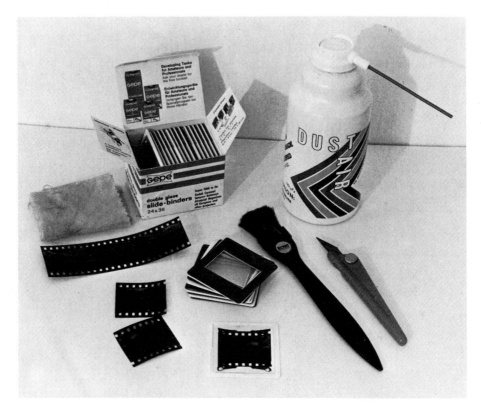

make, (a) no slide can buckle, and (b) after the first has been focused, it follows that all slides will be in focus.

The best fully automatic projectors have other refinements, including a built-in shutter that covers the gate to provide black-out between slides, as nothing is more disturbing than a sudden flash of white light on the screen. The feature is also found on some semi-automatic models.

Here is the specification for a high-grade, fully automatic projector:

1. 250w 24v halogen lamp, to give a bright screen image at a distance.
2. Choice of wideangle, standard 85–90mm zoom, and other lenses up to 250mm focal length, for large audiences. Unless the projector is designed for the purpose, and has larger-than-average lens mount fitting, it may not be able to accept the longer lenses.
3. Auto-focus.
4. Part-power switch or rheostat control of lamp output. Reduced power is often adequate for medium audiences, and can be switched to full power if a dense slide follows a light one. Part-power operation is also said to prolong lamp life.
5. Remote control slide changing, back

and forth. Long lead.
6. Variable auto-change control. This can be set to change slides automatically, at intervals of about 3sec to 30sec.
7. Black-out between slides.
8. Remote control outlet socket, for linking with recording equipment.

150w or 250w?

150w is amply powerful for all home viewing, and for audiences up to about fifty, with a 150mm lens giving a 5ft screen image. In fact, I once used a 150w projector and an 8ft screen for an audience of a hundred-and-fifty people. The image was just bright enough, but only because the hall was completely blacked out.

However, if you are going to do much lecturing or presenting of shows, you would do well to consider a 250w model, as the extra brightness will make all the difference when you get an unexpectedly large audience, or if the hall is not too dark, or if the 'Exit' signs are particularly bright, or if you go in for pictorial slides of a rather dark nature. For average audiences the projector can be used at reduced power, and switched temporarily to full power when a darkish slide appears on the screen.

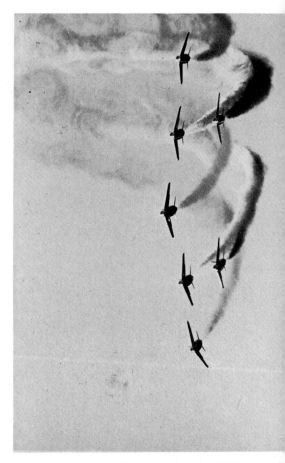

Lenses

Most projectors for home use are provided with a standard lens of 80–90mm, f/2.8, though faster lenses are standard with some more expensive models. At the cheaper end of the market, some lenses are not capable of projecting a flat-field image with sharp detail all over, but all the well-known brands are quite good. It is interesting that with some of the more expensive projectors, you have a choice of two standard lenses, one of which is labelled 'high performance' or some similar name. If you can afford it, get the better lens. First, it usually has an aperture of f/2.5, giving a brighter image. Second, if all your slides are glazed, such a lens will give corner-to-corner sharpness. Unglazed slides invariably buckle, and the best lens in the world cannot project edge-to-edge sharpness when this happens.

If you expect to be projecting to really large audiences, make sure that the projector you buy can be fitted with a lens of sufficient focal length. My own 250mm lenses give a 10ft screen image at 70ft,

adequate for an audience of 500 people, but for Club use a 150mm, or an 85–120mm zoom, is ideal.

Lamps

Nearly all modern projectors take one of two types of halogen lamp: the A1/216 150w 24v, or the A1/223 250w 24v. Many thousands of these are bought worldwide every day, so lamp manufacturers tend to concentrate on their production and they are never in short supply. A local dealer may run out of stock, of course, but these lamps are easily obtained. So it is an advantage to use a projector taking a popular make of lamp.

A few lamps for one or two Continental models, popular in the '60s and early '70s are in short supply, and when found should be purchased in quantity. One of these is the A1/21 100w 12v. If you are really stuck for an old-type lamp, try advertising in a photo magazine. There will always be someone ready to help you out.

Projector lamps have a quartz envelope, and are supplied in a cardboard or foam rubber sleeve. This should be used when inserting the lamp, as finger-acid, which exists even on recently-washed hands, will seriously shorten the lamp life. Life expectancy of a modern lamp is around fifty hours, though many last longer. It is also claimed that lamp life is extended if the projector has half-power or warm-up circuitry, though some experts say this is less true of tungsten halogen lamps than of old-style tungsten lamps. One thing is certain: halogen lamps don't like to be jolted.

A-V facilities

The simplest audio-visual technique is to switch on a record player or tape cassette of your favourite music while you project, turning down the volume when you want to say something. Working with two projectors and a manual fade unit, you can fade one slide into another, and much enhance the aesthetic quality of your show.

More sophisticated units fade by controlling the current to each lamp alternately. The next step up, is by pulsing. By using a recorder such as the little Philips D6920, with the EM1920 slide synchroniser provided with it, an inaudible pulse is added to the tape. When you replay, the slides will be changed automatically.

A more sophisticated A-V twin-projector show uses a 4-track tape. Two tracks have stereo music and other sound material, while a third is pulsed by means of an automatic synchroniser, such as the Pollock Autofade, Electrosonic, Imatronic, and others. The fourth, intervening track, prevents crosstalk between sound and pulse.

Normally, you sit watching the slides and listening to the music, with a synchronising hand unit. On this is a slide-switch, which controls the rate of fade. As the slide is pushed against the end of its track, it adds a slide-change pulse. The recorder is normally linked to a pre-amplifier, then to the automatic synchroniser, from which leads run to the remote control outlet sockets of the two projectors. A great deal of money, and not a little skill, is entailed, but the results can be inspiring.

Mention must be made of a special projector, the Rollei P3801 IR. This has two optical tracks and two lenses, plus a variable built-in fade mechanism and auto slide-change. Although it is more costly than one high-grade conventional projector, it is far less costly than a pair of projectors plus an auto synchroniser and fade unit. Equipped with this, or a pair of conventional projectors, plus the little Philips D6920 with its EM1920 pulsing unit, the amateur has the simplest and most economical equipment for producing a sophisticated show.

Screens

For utmost efficiency, the screen should be of the right material and the audience placed so that people at the end of the front row are not viewing from too acute an angle. Beaded screens have a higher reflectance value than matt screens but, at the same time, are less bright when viewed from an angle. Silver screens are said to have the highest reflectance value

The transparencies of the air hostess and the jets were bound together in a single mount to produce an unusual montage.

of all, but I have never liked the cooling effect they have on intentionally warm slides, such as sunsets and effect interiors.

The typical screen for home projection is hinged to a collapsible stand, and is drawn up from a spring roller. Most of them work well, but on certain makes the screen has a tendency to curl in at the edges when stretched. Check this before buying. Wall screens are convenient as they take up less space and add a useful couple of feet to the lens-screen distance when projecting in a small room. The best of them will lie flat, but avoid like the plague a wall-screen that has a tendency to crease or buckle. A suitable screen size for home use is 4ft 6in. While most cine screens are oblong, a screen for still projection should be square, permitting vertical as well as horizontal slide projection.

Presentation

In one way, photographers are like mothers. They love every single millimetre of emulsion they produce, and are loathe to discard a single slide. You just have to be ruthless when choosing slides for a show. If you shot a certain view from half a dozen angles, choose just one. If you took a selection of portrait expressions, choose just two, and then only if they are really different. During a show, *never* say, "And here's another one." Each and every slide should be necessary. So, Rule No. 1 is to prune your 500 possibles to 50 musts.

Rule No. 2 is to arrange the slides you have chosen into a logical or aesthetically pleasing flow of sequences, and this cannot be stressed too much. A half-hour show needs many hours of preparation. By way of illustration, take the simple story of a trip. Sequences might be (a) departure, (b) arrival, (c) leisure, food and drink, (d) scenery, (e) sport and activities, (f) markets, (g) characters. For aesthetic reasons you may decide to switch some of these around, and mix one sequence with another, but the final arrangement will be simplified if the slides are sorted into strict sequences first.

Rule No. 3 is to maintain artistic continuity. Remember, if you are using fade equipment on two projectors, all slides will have to be horizontal, as you can't fade evenly from horizontal to vertical. Also, remember the effect of showing a dark slide immediately after a bright

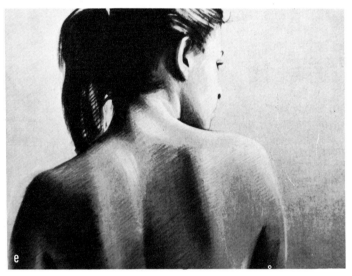

Dissolve techniques in audio-visual work are similar to cine techniques. In this sequence, (a) An out-of-focus shot of the nude, with the brushes sharp. (b) We fade to a sharp nude painting. (c) Fade to half-length painting. (d) How a fade is accomplished, as we fade to (e) a close-up. From colour slides of a painting by artist Lawrence Klonaris.

30min. Make no mistake, that is a long time for an amateur show. Subject matter, presentation and pace, all have to be excellent, if the audience is not to start fidgeting after half an hour.

Harmony

Watch a skilled audio-visual show and you'll see that the slides have been arranged so that colours and shapes blend into each other harmoniously. When arranging your slides ready for final selection, you will probably note several which are predominantly blue—strong skies, people in blue clothes, and so on. For purely aesthetic purposes, you may decide to put these together, as they will fade into each other harmoniously. Similarly, the head of a local character and the bulk of a building or tree may be roughly the same shape, and would again give a harmonious fade. You cannot do this all the time, but watch for the opportunity.

The final fade effects should be borne in mind as much as possible while actually shooting. Try one completely out-of-focus shot of a scene, followed by an in-focus shot, and project them that way. Photograph the same subject in different lighting, at different times of day, ensuring register by using a tripod and carefully noting the framing. This can be magical. Long shots can fade into close-ups taken from the same viewpoint. Keep a face centrally framed (keeping the microprism spot of the focusing screen on the tip of the nose is as good a registering device as any) and shoot different expressions. All these devices add to the harmony and eye appeal of a show, and keep the audience interest.

The oldest cliché in any slide show dealing with travel, is to end with a sunset, and with good reason. It is an ideal ending, and everyone loves a sunset. What is more, a sunset is the ideal subject from which to fade down to a black screen or end title. It doesn't always pay to seek originality, simply for its own sake.

Commentary

A good commentary is factual, audible, sure, entertaining. Let us take those factors one at a time.

Factual: sit down with a pen beforehand, and get your facts right. There is nothing worse than a presenter who mutters, "I think this was taken at Rimini, or was it that place near Venice?"

one—it looks even darker. The same applies to colour. A garish slide excites the eye, while a greenish landscape soothes. Flashing the former on to the screen just after the latter, can cause irritation. On the other hand, and in the right context, it can produce an intentional shock effect.

Rule No. 4 concerns the actual number of slides chosen, which is closely related to the length and pace of the show. Although slides will be on the screen for varying lengths of time, let us presume that you have apportioned 15sec for each. That sounds as though a 50-slide presentation would take only 12½min. No way. By the time you have said your piece(s), and possibly paused a few times to let music and/or sound effects make the right impression, we are talking about

A slide-sorting desk is the best way to sort out your slides when arranging a sequence for a slide show. It also helps you decide which slides will fade harmoniously into others.

Ideally, keep notes while shooting, and don't start mixing slides from different boxes before arranging your sequences, which is a certain path to an unholy loss of both chronology and geography.

Audible: listen to professional presenters on television and radio, and you will notice a skill they share. The voice is never dropped on the last word of a sentence, as it might be in normal face-to-face conversation. Instead, there is a conscious rise in cadence, which the Welsh seem to do in daily converse. This, together with a loud enough delivery, will ensure that the people at the back of the audience (who start the wave of fidgeting that moves down to the front) can hear every word without strain.

If you speak as though you are communicating *only* with the people at the back, everyone will hear. A professional training trick is to listen to yourself speak, which can be done without the aid of a tape recorder. Simply cup the hand around the ear like a forward-facing trumpet, with the thumb and first finger pressed tightly together against the bony area behind the ear. This will conduct the voice waves through the bone, while

the cupped palm guides the sound back into the ear. It is a highly effective way to listen to your speaking voice, and you will instantly be aware of your vocal faults, if any. The two common faults, are to let the voice rise and fall too much, and to fade away at the end of a sentence. Some radio broadcasters sit with their hand cupped like this during a whole session. Most important, never take more than a glance at the screen when standing in front of an audience. This means turning your back to the audience, and spoiling the delivery.

Sure: this is a matter of preparation rather than creativity. Practise what you are going to say until you remember all the facts and the salient points. If this brings a memory of swatting for exams, forget it. We all like looking at our own slides, and we are all interested in our own commentary, so the task is a pleasant one. Your sureness of delivery will communicate itself to the audience and hold their attention.

Lastly, entertaining: remember that the audience is not there to polish your ego, but for you to polish theirs. Foremost among the rules of entertainment is to realise that for you the slides are a memory of things seen, while your audience is seeing them for the first time. An ordinary slide may be interesting to you because it recalls pleasure. By way of example, your seascape may be a visual reminder of the sound of the waves, the smell of ozone and the sense of wellbeing you experienced at the time. The audience, on the other hand, can see and therefore feel only what is on the screen. Thus, when mixing slides and commentary, use commentary to provide what is absent from the screen, and don't waste time describing what can be seen.

Just as important, don't feel compelled to crack schoolboy jokes, unless you have an audience of schoolboys. Even then, make sure the jokes are good. Bad, or laboured jokes, can spoil the best slides. With that final sunset, go for something more fascinating than, ''And so, folks, we leave this land of golden sunsets . . .'' Try silence. However well chosen the music, however interesting the commentary, however good the slides, occasional periods of silence are very telling, and nowhere more telling than during the fadeout of that final, well-chosen, glorious sunset.

22.
Filing

Filing is a chore. The keen photographer would much rather be taking pictures, and developing and printing them, than filing and cross-indexing. And who can blame him? Nevertheless, a sensible filing system is a necessity, not merely because it enables a particular negative, print or slide to be found without a frustrating search, but also because it protects the results of our labours. It has often been said that a filing system is only as good as the person who does the filing, and this is true. Whatever system you adopt, it is essential to start right and keep it going. "One of these days I'll have to get my filing up to date," is a commonly heard complaint, and the only thing that eventually gets filed is the intention.

Over the years I have devised (and kept up!) a filing system that is economical, and which facilitates quick retrieval of negatives, slides and prints. Only once did I let things go, during a six-months period when I was occupied almost daily with professional assignments. Later, it took weeks to bring the system up to date. Now, the extra few minutes occupied with filing after each darkroom session is hardly noticed. You may want to adopt the same system as mine, but even if you already have a filing system of your own, you may still find an improvement or short cut in my methods.

Black & white negatives

My own preference is for negative filing albums, each of which contains thirty semi-transparent leaves of photographic quality. I use Paterson albums, but other makes are available. Each leaf will hold seven strips of six 35mm negatives. This is useful for those occasions when you get more than 36 exposures on a roll. Sometimes I have only part of a roll to file, and the blank sleeves are later filled with other short lengths of negatives. Each sheet is filed facing its related sheet of contact prints, which is my first job at the start of any printing session. Other sheets hold four strips of three 6×6cm negatives, and these are mixed with the 35mm sheets, not filed in separate albums.

Each album is lettered on the spine, A, B, C, and so on. Filing sheets and contacts are consecutively numbered A/1, A/2, A/3, and so on. C/20/5, for example, will be negative No. 5, from sheet 20, of album C.

At one time, I kept a book in which each developed film was given a job number, date, brief description and album reference such as A/7/32. There was also a card file, with subject headings. I still keep up both, but have modified the use of the card file in the light of experience, as we shall see.

Prints

When I make prints for friends, or for reproduction in magazines, these are normally A4 size. Some, such as how-to-do-it sequences, are printed half this size. After a printing session, the reference number is written on the back, in the corner, with a fine-tipped spirit pen. Ordinary biro and felt-tip pens will smear on the back of an RC print.

If used to illustrate a magazine article, the print is sent away, and returned to me from the editorial some weeks later. Naturally, prints made for friends do not come back. At one time, I used to file returned prints, or those still unused, in a hanging foolscap file under such headings as Children, Natural History, Male Portraits, Animals, Landscapes, Seascapes, Girls, and so on. The trouble with this method is that there are too many overlapping categories. One picture might be a landscape with a touch

of sea, whereas a girl studying a butterfly could be filed under Girls or Natural History. This print file rapidly became a mess. Some folders were packed with prints, others contained just one. Arranged alphabetically under subjects, it wasn't always easy to remember a particular designation.

The answer was to reduce the print file to a simple system of letters, A, B, C, and so on, related to the negative albums. For convenience, no more than twenty or so prints are kept in a folder, and when this number is exceeded, a second folder is placed behind the first one. A print marked B/20/36 will be filed before one marked B/26/9, B/26/10 will come immediately after that, and so on.

Retrieval

If somebody telephones and asks for a further copy of a photograph, and can quote the reference from the back, all I have to do is take down the album and turn to the right sheet. If they do not have the original print, and cannot therefore quote a reference, they can usually remember roughly when the picture was taken. Then, I refer to the chronological job book.

What happens when I need a certain picture to illustrate an article—a picture taken ages ago, and which might be in any of five albums? This is where my modified card index system comes in handy. Early on, I tried to cross-reference every picture I took, and the card index soon became far too complex. A single picture might be cross-referenced under London, Cityscape, Portrait, Available Light, Rain, and even the name of a person modelling for me. Much later, I might have forgotten all those references, and start searching fruitlessly under Piccadilly.

Nowadays, I index people's names, place names, and certain broad categories which I know may be useful for illustrative purposes. These include such references as Cloud Effects, Farms, Pastoral, Athletics, Snow. The trick is not to index every picture, but just an album/sheet reference. When that sheet is turned to, the contact sheet will show several associated pictures taken at the same time, and a choice can be made.

Usually, I remember if a print has already been placed in the print file, which saves the trouble of making another. As the print file tallies with the album/sheet reference, it takes only moments to check. Occasionally, I get ideas for an illustrated article simply by browsing through the albums, and for this purpose a cross-index can also be

Slides can be selected direct from the file sheets for a particular show, and later returned to the file for safety.

A government surplus filing cabinet is ideal for a large collection of slides, which can be filed under subjects. For smaller collections, albums are obtainable into which the filing sheets can be clipped.

helpful. If I find a good snow picture, for example, a reference to the Snow card will indicate where other contact sheets containing snow pictures are to be found.

Filing slides

As most of my colour work is for projection in audio-visual shows, and for magazine and book reproduction, I use slide film. Only rarely do I shoot negative colour, and these negatives and colour prints are filed together with my black & white work.

Undoubtedly, the best way to file slides is in hanging files. Transparent sheets are available which will hold twenty or more 35mm transparencies in standard 2×2in mounts. The sheet can be lifted from the file and held to the light, so that all the slides can be seen instantly. This is far easier than ploughing laboriously, one slide at a time, through box after box.

Many of your slides will be arranged

in magazines, for showing, and once a good selection has been assembled, there is little point in breaking a magazine down and returning the individual slides to a filing system. Your job book and card index will help locate a particular slide, whether this is in a magazine or the file.

Whether or not to keep a separate job book and card index for slides, will depend on how many pictures you take. If your output is in the region of twenty or so films a year, separate indexing is probably unnecessary, but for greater quantities will make the job of retrieval much easier.

With slides, unlike negatives, there are no contact sheets to be examined, which means that the slides themselves will be handled far more often than negatives. This is another good reason to use hanging files. Each slide is protected in a separate sleeve and does not have to be removed for examination. Unglazed slides kept in boxes, especially those supplied by the processor, are at risk of being scratched every time they are sorted through. Magazines should always be stored in proper magazine boxes, to prevent the accumulation of dust and the risk of abrasion.

Individual slide mounts of plastic or metal can be referenced with a fine-point spirit pen, and any fine pen will do for card mounts. If a slide is sent away, for magazine illustration or to a competition, it should be clearly identified as your property. With card mounts, your name and address, and even a title, can be written on in ink, but for plastic and metal mounts it is best to use the small self-adhesive labels obtainable in sheets at any stationers. Make sure the mount surface is clean and greasefree, and that the label sticks flat. If the end of a self-adhesive label folds over, it can easily stick in the gate of a projector, or to another slide.

Slides which are submitted to magazines and competitions should never be in glazed mounts. However well packed, there is always the risk of breakage. This can not only ruin the transparency, but many an unfortunate secretary has had bloodied fingers caused in this way. Protection is best afforded by sealing the slide in a 6×6cm or 6×9cm glassine envelope. Unlike negative filing sheets, glassine envelopes are crystal clear, and editor or judges can evaluate a slide without removing it from the envelope. A name and address label can be stuck in a corner, for extra identification.